VOICES FROM
TIANANMEN
SQUARE

BEIJING SPRING AND
THE DEMOCRACY MOVEMENT

This book is dedicated to the memory of all those who lost their lives
in Tiananmen Square, Beijing
June 1989

How flourishing the grasses on the prairies are!
They grow and wither year after year.
The wildfire can only burn out some of them,
But they will come to life again when the Spring breeze blows.

Bai Juyi

edited by Mok Chiu Yu and J. Frank Harrison

VOICES FROM
TIANANMEN
S Q U A R E

BEIJING SPRING AND
THE DEMOCRACY MOVEMENT

Introduction by George Woodcock

**BLACK
ROSE
BOOKS**

Montréal-New York

BLACK ROSE BOOKS No. S 142

Hardcover ISBN: 0-921689-59-4
Paperback ISBN: 0-921689-58-6

Canadian Cataloguing in Publication Data
Main entry under title:
  Voices from Tiananmen Square

Includes bibliographic references.
ISBN 0-921689-59-4 (bound).--
  ISBN 0-921689-58-6 (pbk.)
  1. China--History--Tiananmen Square Incident, 1989--Sources.
  2. Student movement--China--Interviews. I. Yu, Mok Chiu II.
  Harrison, J. Frank

DS779.32.V64 1990   951.05'8   C90-090136-5

Cover design: Marie-José Chagnon
Design and Layout: Nat Klym

BLACK ROSE BOOKS
Editorial Offices
3981 St-Laurent Boulevard, Suite 444
Montréal, Québec H2W 1Y5 Canada

U.S. Orders
BLACK ROSE BOOKS
340 Nagel Drive
Cheektowaga, New York, 14225 USA

BLACK ROSE BOOKS
Mailing Address
P.O. Box 1258
Succ. Place du Parc
Montréal, Québec H2W 2R3 Canada

TABLE OF CONTENTS

Response of the Workers

Disillusionment in the Party

The Doubts of Soldiers

The Intellectuals Comment

A Chinese Solidarity in the Making

SECTION FOUR: INTERVIEWS WITH THREE LEADING PERSONALITIES

SECTION FIVE: WITNESSES TO THE MASSACRE

PREFACE

Tiananmen Square is no European Piazza. More than 100 acres in size, and capable of holding hundreds of thousands of people, it is the centre of a city of ten million people, which is the capital of the People's Republic of China (PRC), Beijing. It is the symbol of China and Chinese government in the same way that Red Square and the Kremlin symbolise the USSR, and Washington with its white monuments the USA. Around the periphery of Tiananmen Square, and in the streets and avenues leading away from it, are the buildings which house the personnel who lay claim to the governance of 1.1 billion people, about a fifth of the entire human race. Therefore, the Democracy Movement of April-June 1989, centred on the Square, can be said to have been of world historic proportions. That is certainly what the writers of documents given here thought, and they are probably right.

In this collection of writings, numerous Beijing place-names are mentioned. The reader will avoid confusion if s/he remembers that the events centred upon **Tiananmen Square**, in which is situated the huge **Monument to the People's Heroes** and the **Mausoleum** of Mao Zedong. On the west side of the Square is the **Great Hall of the People**, the meeting place for government bodies, including the National People's Congress. On the east side of the Square is the **Museum of Chinese History**, which is attached to the **Museum of the Revolution**. At the north end of the Square is the reviewing stand which stands over the entrance to the **Forbidden City**, now the Palace Museum. To the west of the Forbidden City is the **Zhongnanhai** compound for senior government and party personnel, the main entrance of which is called **Xinhuamen**. Running east-west (south of Zhongnanhai and the Palace Museum, through the north end of the Square) is the major thoroughfare, **Changan** Avenue. A mile to the east on Changan, past the **Beijing Hotel**, is the **Jianguomen** overpass. Just over a mile to the west is the **Xidan** intersection, then the **Fuxingmen** overpass after another mile or so, then **Muxidi** bridge, and then the **Military Museum** over four miles west of the Square. These were the killing grounds of Beijing in 1989.

The documents have no single ideological theme. However, many pieces directly reflect the immediate and passionate hatred for an entrenched regime indifferent to the thoughts, needs and desires of the larger population. Stimulated by the students, that population joined them in their millions, and the Student Movement of 1989 became a Popular Movement. One also catches sight of the divisiveness and distrust that develops between those who are allies in the struggle against authoritarianism, but who differ deeply on questions of tactics. We even see Chai Ling, a leader of the hunger strikers in Tiananmen Square, accusing fellow students of trying to kidnap herself and her husband. The situation was nothing if not complicated, with numerous elements and organizations involved.

Central to it all, however, was the assertion that civilised human beings must control their own lives, and that this will only happen if the *masses* (not just the students) make the power of the State subordinate to their practical needs. We see in response to this revolution in the making, reactionary and desperate military violence. The term, "fascist," was given renewed meaning as the communist party elite of a so-called socialist State used bloody domination with the single purpose of maintaining that State (and their associated privileges) against the challenge of the people.

The conservative and authoritarian element of the leadership of the People's Republic of China, led by President Yang Shangkun and Premier Li Peng, ordered dependable forces in the People's Liberation Army to kill the students and demonstrators of the capital of China, which they did on the night of June 3-4, 1989. We do not know how many they killed, but at least 3000, with some of the documents contained here suggesting figures of as high as 7000. The new reign of terror must horrify us, though it may not surprise us. Meanwhile, we should note that Mr. Gorbachev has distanced himself from the events in order to promote rapprochement with the Chinese State after the years of the Sino-Soviet dispute; and the American State Department continues its China policy of cozy compatibility. The modern State, be it represented by the opaque neo-conservatism of a disoriented George Bush, or the frantic scrambling of a Gorbachevian *perestroika*, consciously and deliberately ignores ethical principle for reasons of State. Therefore, we should remember that these voices of China are aligning themselves with neither East nor West, but presenting the need for a politics against the State, which is the only circumstance in which politics can have a truly human face.

There are numerous references to events in Chinese history in these writings, and in order to facilitate an easy understanding, the following brief summation of major events in modern Chinese history is provided for the reader.

1919: May Fourth Movement organised following a mass demonstration by students against the post-war delivery of Chinese territory to Japan, even though China had been a member of the anti-German alliance during World War I.

1921: Formation of the Chinese Communist Party (CCP). From now until 1949 the communists were either in an uneasy alliance with the Nationalist Party (Guomindang), or in open conflict with it.

1935-1945: War between the Chinese Republic and imperialist Japan.

1949: Foundation of the communist regime on mainland China: the People's Republic of China (PRC).

1950-1953: Korean War in which the army of the PRC was involved against the forces of the United Nations (principally the USA).

1956: The Hundred Flowers Movement. The short-lived freedom given to intellectuals to criticise the regime.

1958: The Great Leap Forward. The attempt, initiated by Mao Zedong, to establish the economic and organizational basis of communism through an enthusiastic commitment to collective goals by the masses. Of particular note was the creation of Communes for the 80% of the population which lived in rural China, which sought to integrate every factor of life within a single administrative framework. They were eventually dismantled in 1982.

1960: Withdrawal of Soviet technicians from China. For the next twenty-five years the relationship between the PRC and the USSR is summarised by the term, "Sino-Soviet Dispute."

1966-1976: The Great Proletarian Cultural Revolution. Mao Zedong initiated a massive purge of the Chinese hierarchy in order to guarantee his predominance in the Chinese Communist Party (CCP) and, thereby, the PRC. The youth of China were recruited by Mao as a vanguard force in his struggle, with stability imposed by the People's Liberation Army (PLA) after widespread social disorders developed in 1967.

1971: Lin Biao, Minister of Defence, and Mao Zedong's supposed heir apparent, was shot down whilst fleeing the country after an attempt to assassinate Mao and take power.

1976: Death of Premier Zhou Enlai. Prior to his death he had introduced the policy of the "Four Modernizations" (industry, agriculture, the military, science and technology), aimed at a calculated, technically-based economic modernization of the PRC by the year 2000. This became official policy, supported by economic reforms, when Deng Xiaoping became dominant two years later. At Zhou's funeral, on April 5th, a massive demonstration indicated opposition to the Cultural Revolution. During the days following further demonstrations were repressed by the authorities, and these events came to be known as the April Fifth Movement.

1976: Death of Mao Zedong, following which Deng Xiaoping became the dominant personality in Chinese politics. Famous for the phrase, "It doesn't matter what colour the cat is, as long as it catches mice," Deng typified an anti-Maoist, anti-egalitarian, economic pragmatism. The authoritarian egalitarianism of Maoism ended with the arrest of the so-called Gang of Four — Jiang Qing (Mao's widow), Wang Hongwen, Zhang Chunqiao and Yao Wenyuan — who were submitted to a huge show trial four years later.

1978: The 3rd plenum (i.e., meeting) of the Central Committee elected by the Eleventh Party Congress (of 1977), where an economic reform programme permitting a significant private sector was promoted.

1978: Xidan-Democracy Wall Movement. Through the winter of 1978-1979, many big character posters appeared, often criticising public officials and public policy. Brought to an end in March, 1979. The high profile dissident, Wei Jingsheng, was the chief victim of the crackdown.

1979: Deng Xiaoping's declaration of the Four Cardinal Rules, prohibiting all activities, i) against socialism, ii) against proletarian dictatorship, iii) against leadership by the party, and iv) against Marxism-Leninism and the Thought of Mao Zedong. This represented the dominant line in the ruling elite, which was a refusal to introduce socio-political reforms to supplement on-going economic reforms.

1982: The 12th Party Congress creates the Central Advisory Commission as an institutional "retirement home" for the senior party personnel. The body became a centre of reactionary intrigue against reform leaders of the CCP (such as Hu Yaobang and Zhao Ziyang) and social movements outside the party.

1983: The Chinese Communist Party (CCP) announced a crackdown on "spiritual pollution" and "bourgeois liberalization."

1984: Deng Xiaoping announced an "open-door" policy to encourage foreign investment in the PRC.

1987: Following student demonstrations in the final weeks of 1986, an "anti-bourgeois liberalization" campaign was promoted by the CCP through its newspaper, the *People's Daily*. The General Secretary of the CCP, Hu Yaobang, was forced to resign.

1988: The Central Committee of the CCP endorsed Premier Li Peng's policy of slowing down economic reform, and delaying price reforms for at least two years. This was a serious setback to the plans of General Secretary of the CCP, Zhao Ziyang.

1989: April 15 — death Hu Yaobang, which became the stimulus for the 1989 Democracy Movement, the details of which can be found in the first section of this volume.

The reader should refer to the following list of abbreviations and positions in the hierarchy of China. I have also provided notes for clarification at those points in the documents where it seemed useful. In this volume,

ASUBU refers to the Association of Students' Unions of Beijing Universities, which was the major spontaneous organization that developed during the period, uniting the activities of the seventy-plus institutions of higher education in the city.

CCP refers to the Chinese Communist Party, the ruling party of the PRC which is, effectively, a one-party State.

NPC refers to the National People's Congress, constitutionally the highest legislative authority, but effectively controlled by the CCP, as is its Standing Committee and the State Council, which it elects.

PLA refers to the People's Liberation Army, which includes the forces of the navy and the air force. It is controlled by the CCP through the Military Commission of the party, chaired at the time by Deng Xiaoping.

PRC refers to the People's Republic of China, which is mainland China, governed from Beijing.

It is the Standing Committee of the Political Bureau (Politburo) of the Central Committee of the CCP that decides the direction that China will take, supported by a party hierarchy which "benefits" from its power. The only opposition, the only alternative, was "in the Square." They crushed the alternative temporarily by persuading the PLA that the students and citizens of Beijing were criminals. However, as the central Europeans have shown, and we see clearly in these pages that Chinese eyes are on that part of the globe, even neo-fascist regimes have their military limits when the mass of citizens choose to disobey. In the PRC it is a question of whether or not the discontent of China's relatively sophisticated urban population will become the consciousness of the broader mass of citizens; and, as in all States, to what degree the military begins to identify with the people as opposed to the regime, thereby at least neutralising itself as a political force.

Finally, I would like to acknowledge those friends and comrades from Hong Kong who have participated in this project as gatherers of information and translators of the original documents: Dennis Lau, Amy Chow, Yuen Che Hung, Edna

Lam, Subrina Chow, C. Weng, Mary Chan, Winky Po, Evian Wong, Alice Ng, Helen Choi, May Yuen, Alice Chan, Olivia and Vincent, Jude Hui, and Susan Ho. Meanwhile, in Canada, the value of Ann-Marie Swarbrick's patient proof-reading was immeasurable.

J. Frank Harrison

FOREWORD

There are a number of things I now remember sadly and with a little incredulity about the China in whose northern regions, up to the Gobi desert, I travelled in 1987. One was the way in which people I encountered talked with a kind of reserved satisfaction about the freedoms that appeared to have entered in many directions into Chinese life during the 1980s. Surprisingly often they ended in a kind of undertone: "we only hope *it* will last."

I also remember the coded circumlocutions in which political matters that should not be discussed openly were presented. Classic Chinese figures had now — after the end of the Cultural Revolution — settled into their old niches, and Confucius once again represented authority, so that a remark in favour of Lao Tzu would be regarded — and often received with broad grins — as an oblique hit at the Party.

One piece of coding I found particularly directed towards me. Nowhere was I directly asked about my political attitudes, nor was it even openly said that they were known to the people I encountered. Instead what I found to be a standard coded circumlocution was applied to me. "You are the Canadian Ba Chin." Ba Chin, of course, is that marvellous survivor Li Pei-kan, the devoted anarchist I knew through correspondence in the mid-1940s, and who since then has gone through prison after prison and struggle session after struggle session as a dissident, and always emerged to resume his role as one of China's leading men of letters and a notable novelist. Half a century ago and more, he was already translating Kropotkin into Chinese, and then he adopted the pen name he still uses — Ba being the first syllable of Bakunin's name and Chin being a Chinese adaptation of the last syllable of Kropotkin's. In his eighties he had become a symbol of steadfastness among the younger writers. I was flattered by the identification, and pleased by the subtle way in which so many people seemed to be expressing their tolerance for anarchist ideas. Perhaps I should have paid more attention to the fact that even in 1987 such ideas were *evoked* but *never mentioned, never named.* Tolerance — or daring — had not yet gone so far.

The daring would emerge — and counter to it a return to open autocracy — in the China of 1989, when the students and many of the ordinary people of Beijing acted as most anarchists merely intend to act, by fighting magnificently and non-violently in their fifty days of demonstrations for freedom of speech, assembly, political life, while the authorities cancelled years of apparently increasing tolerance in a few hours on the night of the 3-4 June, when the cruel gerontocrats who had seized control of the Communist Party and the People's Liberation Army ordered the massacre of the students in Tiananmen Square and then tried by propaganda lies, like the rulers in *1984,* to wash their crimes into the memory holes of history.

So the "it" of 1987, the promise of freedom, did not endure, and old Ba Chin, who had predictably expressed his support and admiration for the students, was imprisoned once again, though like Malatesta in Mussolini's Italy and Tolstoy in Tsarist Russia, he was considered a figure whose moral stature made it impossible to be done away with, and he was finally released.

We need all the witnesses we can get to the events leading up to that June night in 1989 which may in the end be seen as one of the turning points of history. There have already been some useful eyewitness accounts by foreign writers, of which perhaps the most immediate is *Tiananmen Square,* 1989 by the Canadian journalists Scott Simmie and Bob Nixon. But such narratives, though they may be vivid in their evocation of what it all looked and sounded and even smelt like, and in their highly sympathethic accounts of people engaged in passionate, self-denying struggle for a future many of them did not live to see, are still the accounts of observers, not of participants. In *Voices from Tiananmen Square* you will hear of the struggle in the echoing words of the Chinese people who were involved, workers as well as students.

I do not know whether one can think of the events in Beijing in May and June 1989 as an actual revolution. They may have been revolutionary in promise, but they never reached the boiling point of a complete uprising of the people, and only the scared rulers saw them as a movement setting out to destroy the government. The students who participated, and the workers and common people who supported them were concerned primarily with relatively limited aims — mainly establishing dialogue, as they termed it, on basic democratic rights.

In the long run, of course, the Party bosses may have been right in their fears, as the parallel though later events in eastern Europe suggest. Many famous revolutions have begun with limited aims — taxes in English seventeenth and the American eighteenth centuries, bread in France in 1789, war weariness in Russia in 1917. The real revolutionary ideologues and intriguers, with their plans to reconstitute society and seize power, are usually a manipulative, late-coming minority, though at times specific grievances are accompained, as they were in 1848, by a widespread sense that it is time to sweep away the rubbish of outdated institutions. The Chinese uprising seems to have been rather of this kind, starting off on limited issues of free speech, but sustained by an awareness that society has become corrupt and can be healed only by a change in political relations.

Most movements of this kind have turned out great masses of literature which by its very nature is fragmentary. The pamphlets of the Levellers and the Diggers emerged in the English 1640s, and there was a vast production of leaflets, manifestos and posters in the French revolution of 1789, out of which Kropotkin largely wrote his study of the movement from below, *The Great French Revolution.* 1848, The Commune, 1917 in Russia, the Spanish Civil War, all produced their popular literature tied to the events of the time, and student protest movements in China have always been characterized by a great activity in posters and wall newspapers, as well as leaflets passed from hand to hand. Much of *Voices from Tiananmen Square* consists of such manifestos, and most of them reveal one of the important aspects of the 1989 movement; that political ideologues were not in control, though the protesters were not politically unsophisticated; how could they have been after the years of indoctrination against which they were reacting?

You will not find much of the personal and intimate here; these people are not concerned with impressionistic evocation, but with calling a society to moral order. Three or four people from among the student leaders appear as recognizable individuals in the handful of interviews that are offered, but nobody writing here has really had the tranquillity to reflect on his or her feelings during the days of insurrection. You will learn a great deal about their ideas, about their motivations, about their comprehension of events, and you will get a sense of the idealism that prompted their extraordinary endurance and audacity. Here they are, urging, defending, and to hear them doing so brings their cause to life. One day, one hopes, some of their survivors will be able to tell the personal drama of it all, as I heard it in tones of exaltation and grief from one participant who spent two hours telling me what he had experienced and felt; I can neither name nor describe him, for that might endanger others.

Voices from Tiananmen Square is material for history rather than history itself. It is concentrated in Beijing, and makes passing references only to what went on in other centres. It gives little indication of what effect the news from the captial may have had on the peasants, who still make up three quarters of China's population. And inevitably there is nothing said about what was going on among China's ruling groups except in so far as it directly affected the students and their fellow protesters.

Yet in any final analysis of events in Tiananmen Square the struggle that went on simultaneously in the centres of power has to be considered, since the challenge of the students set it going. It was a struggle not merely within the party but also within the army, and between the party and the army, in which the former gained in power to such an extent that we may be looking at a Napoleonic phase in Chinese history. Very soon after the student demonstrations started, rumours began to circulate regarding differences within the PLA, with the Beijing command opposing violent action against the protesters. The Beijing command in fact was the last to formally approve Li Peng's declaration of martial law. Its commander received a sentence of eighteen years imprisonment for having booked himself into a hospital rather than direct an offensive in Tiananmen Square. There are even persistent reports that six or seven lesser generals in the same army were summarily executed. What appears to be certain is that the PLA was captured by the faction headed by Yang Shangkun, the President of China, a Great Marcher as aged as Deng, who emerged from ceremonial retirement to play a key role in the resolution of the crisis. Yang is not only the head of the Chinese State; he is also nepotistic leader of a clan of high offi- cers — sons, sons-in-law and nephews. One of these kinsmen com- manded the troops who perpetrated the massacre in Tiananmen Square. They were brought down from the isolation of North-easter- ly Shenyang province, where for weeks they had been isolated and indoctrinated with hardline propaganda. When they were released to do their work on the night of the 3rd June they had been heavily inoculated with amphetamines and were no longer responsible human beings.

By accepting the aid of the hardline faction which won con- trol in the army, the Communist Party in China has entirely lost face, and it is now the generals with their allies in the security police who are in effective control of China. Deng has become the feeble figurehead of the military, and both the leading poltical figures in China today, Premier Li Peng and party General Secre- tary Jiang Ximen are men without power. Li cut away his own popular following (such as it was) and his base within the party when he obeyed Yang and proclaimed martial law; when his own fall comes he will have no friend. Jiang, the party boss of Shan- ghai, had no base elsewhere, and it was for his dispensibility that he was chosen. When Deng dies either or both can be pushed aside without fear of effective protest within the party or else- where. That, of course, brings us round to the fate of Xhao Xiy- ang, of whom we have recently heard so little. Since he is apparently not dead, and his party membership has not been withdrawn, he is almost certainly being kept as a high-grade recy- clable, ready to assume the appropriate role when the People's Liberation Army decides, like its Rumanian counterpart, to re- emerge in the guise of the Army for Liberating the People. Such populist initiatives are entirely within the Napoleonic tradition that now rules China.

One thing is certain, as *Voices from Tiananmen Square* suggests: The people of Beijing have gone through a process of radical politi- cal education and they are unlikely to forgive or forget Li Ping and

his kind. One day these people will act and speak again, and perhaps, as happened before in China — their voices will carry what we
metaphorically term the Mandate of Heaven.

George Woodcock

INTRODUCTION

From the moment of its foundation in 1921, the CCP has always structured itself along hierarchical lines. It assimilated all the forms, techniques and mentality of a bureaucracy. Its membership was schooled in obedience, and taught to revere the leadership which, in its own turn, adopted habits of command, manipulation and egomania. On winning power in 1949, they became the new bosses, setting up a ruthlessly exploitative and repressive bureaucratic system.

The party also took power in a country that was economically backward, a semi-feudal and semi-colonial society that was ravaged by imperialism. The May Fourth Movement of 1919 had sought a path of salvation in "science and democracy." The Marxist-Leninist-Stalinist dogma was not seen to contradict that policy, its anti-colonial and dialectical interpretation of history being singularly appealing to impoverished victims of imperialism. A Marxist-Leninist revolution was expected to revolutionise the social structure, and unleash great productive forces, resolving thereby the problems of poverty and dependency in a proletarian democracy of "the toiling masses."

However, the 1949 revolution had nothing in common with a genuine socialist revolution. The CCP took control of the State through its command of a peasant army. Having gained that control of the State, the only conceivable policy for the Leninist bureaucracy was to impose a regime of ruthless exploitation and austerity over the working people. Economic development rested on the most primitive methods of extracting surplus value. In the countryside, millions of peasants and semi-proletarians were put to work on huge construction and irrigation projects, built almost with bare hands. In the cities, workers were forced to labour for long hours for extremely low wages, strikes were banned, and mobility between jobs limited. The Leninist bureaucracy became a new class, controlling a new mode of production — one in which capital was monopolistically-controlled by the bureaucrats.

Establishing this system took almost the first ten years of communist rule under the direction of Mao Zedong. It also occurred in an environment of internal party debate and power struggles, that have characterised communist rule since its very inception.

Faced with the task of "socialist construction" Mao and his supporters believed that they must bring about the monopolistic control of all capital as soon as possible. They also believed that they did not need technical experts to achieve and operate the system. The Maoist goal was for the dominance of a hierarchy of dedicated and obedient communists, not a "techno-bureaucracy."[1] Mao did not want to see intellectuals playing an increasingly important role, and was particularly adamant against scientists and professionals taking up managerial positions, and separating the party from the people. On the other hand, Liu Shaoqi felt that a certain degree of private capitalism should be allowed, at least for a period of time; and Zhou Enlai argued for the need of techno-bureaucrats in addition to party bureaucrats. Deng Xiaoping was also in the latter camp, which suffered a major setback during 1956 and 1957, when, following an invitation to criticise, hundreds of thousands of intellectuals were persecuted as "rightists" after responding to the invitation.

Generally speaking, Mao was in command from 1949 to 1958. However, his influence was reduced at the end of 1958 because of the massive confusion caused by the Great Leap Forward. At that point, Liu Xiaoqi and Deng Xiaoping introduced a series of policies creating an environment more favorable to the techno-bureaucrats. However, in 1966 Mao initiated the Great Proletarian Cultural Revolution, again reversing the trend; and Maoists were able to dominate policy-making in China until his death in 1976. China was led down the road of a "feudalist social-fascist dictatorship," in which an explicit and demonstrable total subordination to the ideas of Mao and the leadership of his supporters was the condition of life for every Chinese.

Maoist rhetoric, particularly during the days of the 1966-1976 Cultural Revolution, sounded libertarian, and many socialists throughout the world accepted it totally and uncritically, believing that Mao was successfully building a self-managed socialist paradise. It was claimed that Mao was eliminating the three main contradictions in society: between town and country, between workers and peasants, and between manual and mental labour. However, the people of China indicated their unequivocal rejection of Mao's way in April 1976, and how they celebrated when the Gang of Four were arrested! For the reality was that, in Mao's China, the mass of workers and peasants were but slaves of the Leninist bureaucracy, not permitted to run their own lives.

That bureaucracy was obviously privileged, the more so the higher up you looked. They had special stores, luxurious apartments, chauffeured cars, with their children getting educational preference, travel abroad, and access to the best jobs. As for the universities, political loyalty rather than ability became the basis of entrance to institutions where lecturers were not learned professors, but politically-reliable soldiers, workers and peasants. Expertise gave way to toadying, wisdom to political fanaticism. Anyone who complained or criticised was accused of being bourgeois—including the workers who had to suffer miserable wages and working conditions.

Maoist "libertarianism" was never more than rhetoric!

The internal party conflict could be seen developing again in 1973 when "the Number Two capitalist roader" (Liu had been Number One, until his death in 1969), Deng Xiaoping, was reinstated in the hierarchy, after being purged early on in the Cultural Revolution. He was closely associated with Premier Zhou Enlai, one of China's most efficient bureaucrats, who was never trusted by the Maoists. The "Four Modernizations" (of agriculture, industry, science and technology, and defence) was the Zhou-Deng line, not liked by the Maoists because of its promise to raise the authority of intellectual techno-bureaucracy. An "anti-Confucius" movement was begun by the Maoist faction, with Zhou as the prospective target. Zhou cleverly diverted it into an "anti-Lin Biao" campaign, and its energy was spent attacking a man who had been dead since 1971.

Then, in 1976, the people demonstrated in the April Fifth Movement. This led to the dismissal of Deng Xiaoping, reported in the
People's Daily as follows:

> *Early in April a handful of class enemies, under the guise of com-
> memorating the late Premier Zhou during the Ching Ming festi-
> val, engineered an organised, premeditated and planned
> counter-revolutionary political incident at Tiananmen Square in
> the Capital... Openly hoisting the ensign of supporting Deng
> Xiaoping, they frenziedly directed their spearhead at our great
> leader Chairman Mao... On the proposal of our great leader
> Chairman Mao, the Political Bureau unanimously agrees to dis-
> miss Deng Xiaoping from all posts both inside and outside the
> party while allowing him to keep his party membership so as to
> see how he will behave in the future.*

This is how the Leninist bureaucracy dealt internally with the
questions raised by a spontaneous demonstration of the people,
which they had brutally repressed, killing at least 2000 people.

Acutely aware of the unpopularity and ambition of the Maoist
Gang of Four, when Mao died in September, 1976, Hua Guofeng en-
gineered a palace coup removing them, and bringing Deng back into
the ruling circle. Deng's Four Modernizations policy had substantial
support both inside and outside the party, as an alternative to the
deprivations of the Cultural Revolution. Deng's supporters, Hu Yao
Bang and Zhao Ziyang, replaced Hua at the head of the CCP. In addition, those purged during the Cultural Revolution were rehabilitated, including many intellectuals, scientists and artists, in order to
better implement economic reforms required by the modernization
programme. The intellectuals and scientists were assured that, as
brain workers, they were also proletarians, and would not suffer further oppression for their intellectual independence from the CCP.
The Academy of Sciences confirmed a reduction of party controls,
and political education received less emphasis in the education system. Emphasis was now to be placed on technical expertise, with
many students being sent overseas to acquire it.

In the area of industrial management, material incentives, work
discipline, and professionalization were the order of the day. The
distinction between workers and management was re-emphasised,
with the role of political workers reduced and subordinated to that

of the techno-bureaucrats. The adoption of capitalist methods of organization and financing was taken as a mark of progress.

We should remember, however, that Deng was as much a Leninist as any other member of the CCP. The leadership role of the party was never questioned. The State machinery, the PLA, the trade unions and other mass organizations all continued to be subjected to the party's absolute leadership. Rural communities and industrial enterprises, schools and research institutes, were all to be led by the party. The discipline of democratic centralism was to be enforced in the party itself, with the individual obeying the organization, the minority obeying the majority, the subordinate obeying the superior, and the whole party obeying the Central Committee.

It was a rigid hierarchy; yet one which was instructed not to interfere in the day to day operations of the economy, and thus was less domineering than under Mao. Moreover, with a broader array of books, films, art and literature of all kinds, traditional and modern, and with the introduction of a new penal code, the perpetual presence and domination of the party in all spheres of life seemed less evident, even though it was unquestioned.

In this situation, the intellectuals were placed in a situation where they did become a class of techno-bureaucrats, encroaching upon the power of the party bureaucrats. This techno-bureaucracy began to reap the rewards of its elite position, gaining superior access to goods and services.

The techno-bureaucrats were not the only new class to be generated by Deng's policies; for his strategy of modernization also involved a de-monopolization of the economy (i.e., introducing a private sector with market relations determining prices). China developed both rural and urban entrepreneurs, as well as an identifiable group of speculators.

In the agricultural sector the large communes introduced back in 1958 were at last entirely dismantled. The so-called "responsibility system" [2] appealed to the self-interest of the peasants. Former production teams divided up the land, farming equipment, and livestock. Then families scrambled after fertilizers and supplies to "go it alone." Indeed, communal fields became family plots, free markets returned and flourished, peasants decided what they would grow and sell, cash crops appeared and side-line rural industries grew up. Peasants, paying a fixed rent for their land, kept all of their income from the sale of products. Some peasants have grown relatively rich (although you can still find starvation in other regions) with marked inequalities obviously developing — and quite acceptable to the Leninists, headed by Deng.

In the cities, similar developments occurred. The market was given a larger role, with profit to be taken as the chief measure of success. Managers were given more independence for economic planning in their enterprises, with the number of State directives substantially reduced. Profits, after deduction of taxes, were to remain with the enterprise for distribution and/or reinvestment. While the State maintained control of major sectors, many State-owned enterprises were rented out to groups and individuals. There was also a growth of a separate private sector, with many privately-owned enterprises, as well as joint stock enterprises developed with the aid of foreign capital. In special economic zones, foreign capitalists were encouraged to invest in new industrial development with the offer of cheap labour, tax incentives, low-priced factory sites, and a docile labour force in a politically-stable situation. Ten years of such policies had created, by 1989, a new class of entrepreneurs, whose interest was the legal guarantee of the right to private property — coexisting with, if not replacing, the system monopolised by the bureaucrats.

The co-existence of market and bureaucratic economies was bound to create problems. Of particular importance was the development of a dual system of prices — the free market price and the price set by the State. The existence of different prices enabled bureaucrats vested with power and information to profit substantially through the simple process of diverting State supplies to the free market. Such activities accentuated already existing shortages and the inflation of prices. When it was decided that the prices of many staples had been set artificially low, the price reform led to a new round of profiteering. The price increases were felt particularly by urban dwellers, who proceeded to demand higher wages, contributing to an inflationary pressure acknowledged by all.

The Student Movement of 1989, therefore, took place within this context of rampant inflation, official profiteering, and authoritarian rule, as the documents in this volume will show. It was the latest form of the corruption and bureaucratic privilege that had been a constant condition of the so-called "socialist" regime for forty years. They had always made use of public funds, and practiced nepotism as a means of establishing a kind of *de facto* system of inheritance. As the economy opened up in the eighties, new opportunities arose. Foreign investors were plagued by large and small officials demanding kick-backs, "gifts," and trips abroad. Many bureaucrats, or their families, including the children of Deng Xiaoping and Zhao Ziyang, were involved in business and trading, using their power and information for personal profit.

They could not be touched, for they controlled the power of the State and the PLA. They put people in prison without trial, and the torture of prisoners was endemic and systematic. Controlling the mass media allowed them to hide the truth and generate false impressions, denying criticism and preventing opposition. There was marginal improvement, as modernization led to relaxed controls; but the power and ruthlessness of the bureaucracy was intrinsic.

Inside the PRC, intellectual opposition to the situation by dissident writers took on a threefold character. These criticisms became visible as the intense pressures towards political conformity were relaxed in the late seventies, but were primarily a response to the continued party dictatorship. They became the arguments of a developing Democracy Movement, which occurred spontaneously in the major cities of China. Underground publications, big character posters, discussion groups and demonstrations were the vehicles by means of which workers, students, and intellectuals reconsidered the condition of their society.

The *first* theoretical tendency was represented by Wei Jinsheng, who argued that the dictatorship of the proletariat has to be abolished and a "liberal democratic" system established.

The *second* tendency was a Marxist-reformist current represented by Wang Xizhe, who wrote four influential essays outlining his position. His "Strive Hard for the Class Dictatorship of the Proletariat" argued that an underdeveloped country could develop into *either* i) a "feudal-socialist" society, if it isolated itself (as China did under Mao), *or* ii) a society of self-managed cooperatives involved in a world market where capitalism was predominant. In the latter case, dictatorship of the party might develop into a dictatorship of the proletariat, with the advancement of the cultural level and managerial competence of the masses. He suggested that Yugoslavia was following the latter path, which the Chinese should seek to emulate, replacing the control of the party, which should limit itself to ideological questions.

In "The Direction of Democracy," Wang emphasised his rejection of bourgeois democracy, but insisted that democracy was an end in itself, not dependent upon specific modes of production, or to be abandoned for reasons of expedience. Arguing in favour of an association of "free human beings," Wang argued for a renaissance of Marxism grounded in a reconsideration of the theory of alienation. Thus, in his essay, "The Dictatorship of the Proletariat is a Humanist Dictatorship," he asserted that the rule of the proletariat would be harmonious, and grounded in mutual affection. Any exploitative society was regarded as contradicting the nature of humanity.

In 1980, "Mao Zedong and the Cultural Revolution" appeared, stating that Mao was a peasant leader, perhaps the greatest in Chinese history, but still peasant. Preoccupied with becoming an emperor, Mao maintained the agrarian nature of Chinese society, promoting an agro-socialism to mobilise the masses in support for him. In contrast, the reform group of Deng Xiaoping received Wang's support as a vehicle of democratization.

The *third* tendency is a radical one, represented by Chen Erjin in his essay, "On the Proletarian-Democratic Revolution." This identified the social systems of countries like the USSR as revisionist — where a bureaucratic-monopolistic class controls the means of production under the title of socialism. China is said to be "at the crossroads," not having yet degenerated to that level, and can move towards either revisionism or socialism. The hierarchy and autonomy of the State, controlled by the Communist Party, might lead to revisionism, against which socialism must wage a life and death struggle. Reformism is a dead end in this struggle, which requires a proletarian democratic revolution.

Neither Wang nor Chen managed to escape from the concepts and analytical orientation of Marxism. However, their presence in China, along with many others like them, reflects the emergence of the question, "Whither China?" The answer to that will necessarily depend upon the attitudes and actions of the major groups and/or classes in Chinese society — techno-bureaucrats, workers, students, intellectuals, party bureaucrats, peasants, urban entrepreneurs, peasant petty-bourgeoisie, etc. Let us consider the major actors.

Concerning the peasantry, who constitute a majority of the population, most of them did not participate in the Democracy Movements of the seventies and eighties. Most peasants also found their situation improved by the responsibility system, although there had been some discontent over rising taxes and the cost of farming materials such as fertilizer. It remains unclear what the future development of the Chinese countryside holds, whether or not it will become more capitalistic, and even merge with entrepreneurs in the urban areas to form a united class front against the State bureaucracy, and demand complete de-monopolization. The new class of independent private producers has good reason to oppose the continued monopoly of economic and political life; and a free enterprise capitalist economy is its goal. Bourgeois, democratic, liberal pluralism provides the model for this new class.

As we saw earlier, Deng's modernization strategy gave an important role to technical experts, who were transformed into techno-bureaucrats. Their goals were not necessarily in conflict with capitalist ideas — unlimited growth, domination of nature, insatiable consumption, etc. — although in capitalist countries their rise had been at the expense of the actual owners of capital. In countries like China, however, the techno-bureaucracy could *either* develop against the ruling party in an alliance with capital, *or* develop in alliance with the party. Mao had distrusted and persecuted the intellectuals, but his policies failed. During the eighties the techno-bureaucrats definitely could be seen as a class in ascendancy. For a while there seemed to be a good relationship between it and the old State hierarchy. To the degree that it was permitted entry into the hierarchy of the State, it finds authoritarianism acceptable; in which context we should note that Zhao Ziyang was surrounded by advisers who toyed with the idea of "neo-authoritarianism," such as is found in Singapore and South Korea, as a model for Chinese development. That champion of Friedmanite market forces, we should remember, was also the creator of a para-military police, specifically designed for coping with social disturbances.

Nevertheless, in 1989, the techno-bureaucrats of China stood for a relaxation of controls and a reduction of the role of the party — particularly in those areas where they have expertise. They supported the 1989 Movement; for the student demands, if met, would have benefitted them. Historically, the majority of Chinese intellectuals have been characterised by their submission to the State; but circumstances now placed them in opposition to the old men standing guard over the monopoly of power which they call "socialist." Deng originally supported them, seeing them as cats who would catch mice, political neutrals who would get the job done; only later coming to see them as devils who might capture the CCP — as was the case in Eastern Europe. So, the party's techno-bureaucrats, symbolised by Zhao Ziyang, had to be stripped of their power.

The Beijing Workers' Autonomous Federation was the major organization of proletarian power that sprang up in the course of the Democracy Movement. Similar workers' organizations also existed in other Chinese cities. The Beijing federation's membership came principally from workers in the steel industry, railroads, airlines, restaurants and service industries. Using their tent in Tiananmen Square as a base, they promoted their demand for a workers' organization that was autonomous of the State. They discussed their practical grievances, including the large wage discrepancies between workers and managers, lack of democracy in the work-place, lack of genuine representation in the policy-making process, poor safety measures and working conditions, and the deterioration of the workers' standard of living over the previous decade.

By the end of May, the Federation had attracted interest and support from other parts of the country, and the organization was hoping to be able "to realise workers' participation in political affairs," demanding the right "to monitor the Communist Party," and seeking workers' control in the assertion that workers "become the real masters of State and collective enterprises." The Beijing Workers' Autonomous Federation thus signalled the possibility of an independent workers' Movement in China, which sadly had too little time to develop. Members of the Federation were right at the front of the crowds when the shooting started; and many members of the organization were killed. The authorities, of course, condemned it as counter-revolutionary; and after the killings anyone associated with it was rounded up by the police. We must recognise, however, that all of this was the experience of an embryonic organization. In 1989, the working class of China was not mobilised as an entire class, and its power was not fully realised.

As for the students, they had been seen as the techno-bureaucrats of the next generation, with a rosy future promised to them. However, like the students in the West in the 1960's, the Chinese students recognised the appalling quality of everyday life in China. Further, Chinese students are themselves materially impoverished, as well as being psychologically, socially and sexually alienated.

There had been a Student Movement from December, 1986, to January, 1987, lasting for more than a month. The largest demonstrations then were in Shanghai, where Jiang Zemin treated the students like children, when he had deigned to speak with them as mayor of the city. Other demonstrations occurred in Beijing, Tientsin, Wuhan, Shenzhen, Kunming, Guangzhou and Nanjing, demanding better conditions for students, democracy and freedom, honest elections, freedom of the press, price controls, and solidarity with student protestors across the nation. Beijing's students were extremely dissatisfied with press reports that claimed that the demonstrations had been initiated by a handful of disruptive elements, and that the students were accused by the authorities of "raising a red flag to attack the red flag," destroying social stability and social unity. The first document issued by the CCP Central Committee for 1987, on January 6th, said that it was necessary to oppose "bourgeois liberalization," and that the struggle must continue for another twenty years.

The 1986-1987 Movement was, therefore, officially regarded as a result of bourgeois liberal ideas, and the lack of a resolute attitude by "certain leading comrades," particularly Hu Yaobang. Hu was soon forced to resign from his position as General Secretary of the CCP. Intellectuals like Fang Lizhi, Wang Ruowang and Liu Binyan were expelled from the CCP for being leading and influential examples of bourgeois liberalism. Party publications called them "capitalist roaders," and a campaign against all who dared voice opposition to the party was organised. Meanwhile, one Shanghai participant wrote,

Our Movement, a spontaneous Movement has ended. However, this is the end of just one phase of development. Our past efforts will not have been wasted if we continue our activities. The Movement has encouraged serious thoughts in every university student. In just a few days we came to understand our society more deeply, and recognise our own strengths and weaknesses... This national Movement of students will undoubtedly contribute to China's historical transformation, its character reflected in its contribution to the democratic consciousness of students, of a generation of Chinese, even of the whole people.

The consensus of the students was, first, that there had been a lot of empty slogans but no concrete demands and, second, that they had not been sufficiently well-organised.

Remembering the Tiananmen revolt ignited by the activities to commemorate Zhou Enlai in April 1976, one should not be surprised that, when Hu Yaobang died on April 15, 1989, the commemorative activities ignited a prairie fire of student revolts, and near revolution. Hu was seen to be one of the rare clean bureaucrats, and a General Secretary who had been open to student demands for democratization. Also, the students, in April, 1989, were already forming organizations and discussion groups. The mood was that something ought to be done in the year marking the seventieth anniversary of the May Fourth Movement, the bicentennial of the French Revolution, and the fortieth anniversary of the foundation of the People's Republic.

However, it would be wrong to over-emphasise the revolutionary intentions (as opposed to consequences) of most of the students. As the documents in this volume demonstrate, they stressed their patriotism. For the most part, they did not demand an overthrow of the bureaucracy, but the creation of a legal opposition. They were not particularly concerned with the plight of the workers, and tended to view their Movement as one which was restricted to students and intellectuals. Happy to be cheered along from the sidewalk during their demonstrations, pleased to be assisted in their attempts to break through police cordons, the students retained a sense of their distinctness, and viewed the rest of society merely as a support mechanism. Even when martial law was declared on May 19th, and the people of Beijing flocked to the streets to prevent the army from entering the city, the students gave little evidence of a desire to broaden their Movement, and unite with the workers. Not until May 25th did the students in Tiananmen Square come up with a strategic proposal to go all out for the support of the workers, and even then they were afterwards sidetracked by debates concerning the date of their departure from the Square.

In the last analysis, we must see the Beijing spring, and the Tiananmen massacre, as evidence of the necessity of a self-conscious unity of interest of the people, rural and urban, against the Leninist State. The students, who in every society are capable of forming the catalyst of social renewal, must inevitably join with other social forces if their actions are to be anything more than an irritant to established authority. The documents in this collection suggest that this was the direction in which the Movement was heading, and that this will be the pattern of future conflicts which must precede the demise of the bureaucratic Chinese State.

As this analysis has shown, the various forces in China do not make for easy predictions concerning the final character of the changes that the Democracy Movement showed to be necessary and inevitable. However, as anarchists, we can hope and struggle for the generation of multiple areas of autonomous self-management and self-government. Therefore, as ever, it is the responsibility of libertarians to remain active in support of a non-capitalist, egalitarian alternative to the historically-defunct Chinese "socialist" State.

Mok Chiu Yu

NOTES
1. This term is from the programme of the Italian Anarchists, who explain it as follows: " The techno-bureaucracy defines itself in the intellectual work corresponding to managerial functions in the hierarchical division of social labour. The 'new bosses' have these functions and from them derive their relative privileges and powers not on account of private ownership rights of the means of production but rather by virtue of a sort of intellectual ownership of the means of production."
2. At the time of writing, this still exists. However, restrictions are being introduced, and the "past tense" is used on the understanding that more changes are likely to occur.

I

THE EVENTS: A CHRONOLOGY[1]

THE 1989 DEMOCRACY MOVEMENT

April 15 (Saturday)

Former General Secretary of the Chinese Communist Party, Hu Yaobang, died of a heart attack. The CCP Central Committee's obituary concluded, "The death of comrade Hu is a great loss to our Party and our people. We must convert our grief into strength, study his selfless and firm allegiance to the party, follow his unceasing dedication to the service of the people, so that under the leadership of the party, we will progress along the path of Chinese socialism."

April 16 (Sunday)

Students and teachers of the various Beijing Universities began putting up posters[2] in memory of Hu Yaobang. Slogans attacking the corruption of the government also began to appear on campuses.

The CCP Central Committee decided to hold Hu's funeral at the Great Hall of the People on April 22nd.

April 17 (Monday)

In the morning, the CCP Central Committee held a meeting in the Great Hall of the People. Wreaths placed by Beijing University students at the Monument of People's Heroes in Tiananmen Square had been removed, to protest which some 3000 Beijing University students marched to Tiananmen Square. Their delegation submitted a petition with seven requests: i) re-evaluation of Hu Yaobang's achievements, ii) rejection of the 1987 "anti-bourgeois liberalization" campaign, iii) freedom of the press, iv) increase of the education budget, v) freedom to protest and demonstrate, vi) publication of the financial holdings of senior government officials, and vii) abolition of the municipal regulations controlling demonstrations in Beijing.

In Shanghai students and citizens began public mourning for Hu Yaobang, also demanding democracy.

April 18 (Tuesday)

Some 5000 students, largely from Beijing University, marched on Tiananmen Square shouting slogans like, "Down with tyranny," "Long live democracy," "Down with official profiteering," and "Down with corruption." Qinghua University students also marched into the Square, breaking through a police cordon in front of the Great Hall to lay a wreath. Students began to sit down in the Square, their number increasing to more than 30,000 by the afternoon, watched over by armed police.

At 10:50 p.m. about 1000 students rushed towards Xinhuamen,[3] trying to present wreaths in honour of Hu Yaobang.

April 19 (Wednesday)

In the early morning about 1000 students went to Xinhuamen to present wreaths and the petition. Armed police formed a blockade, and the crowd tried three times to break through it. Soon there were some 10,000 people shouting, "Down with Li Peng." As the crowd tried to push forward, it clashed with the police. Later, many students reported that they had been beaten up by the police. The authorities stated that the clash had been initiated by people throwing bottles at the police.

Throughout the day students from the various universities came to Tiananmen Square with their slogans and portraits of Hu. By 8:00 p.m. there were over 100,000 people, but the students were well-disciplined, singing the *Internationale* or shouting slogans like, "Down with official profiteering." At night the Monument became a temporary platform and many students and teachers gave speeches on democracy and freedom.

In Shanghai some 3000 students from Fudan University held a rally calling on the Chinese people to unite in the struggle for democracy and freedom.

April 20 (Thursday)

At midnight there were about 20,000 people outside Xinhuamen, while 2000 armed security police formed a barrier. At 2:30 a.m. armed police started using batons to disperse the crowd, which countered with bottles. About 100 students were injured. New China News Agency reported simply that four policemen were injured.

In the absence of action by the official Student Union, Beijing University students called for the formation of an organization responsible for the leadership of all student movements in Beijing. "A letter to all Beijing Universities" declared that mourning for Hu had become a Movement struggling for Democracy, affirming seven points of the petition. Demonstrations and protests were also held in other cities (e.g., Shanghai, Wuhan and Tianjin).

The New China News Agency accused the crowd of shouting "Down with the Communist Party" during the "Xinhuamen Incident."

April 21 (Friday)

A strike declared by the Preparatory Committee of the Solidarity Students' Union of Beijing University students, called to protest the Xinhuamen incident, was followed by other universities. Students from various universities arrived at Tiananmen Square, and by noon there were about 100,000 people there. At 3:00 p.m. some tried to break into the Great Hall of the People, but failed. By the evening, there were over 200,000 people in the Square, including workers and peasants.

Forty-seven scholars (including Yan Jiaqi,[4] Bao Zunxin,[5] Dai Qing,[6]) presented a petition to Zhongnanhai, requesting the government to support the students' Democracy Movement, to stamp out corruption and to re-evaluate earlier democracy movements. The document was rejected, and even thrown to the ground.

In Tianjin hundreds of Nankai University students were prevented from going to Beijing by the university authorities who cancelled their train tickets. Impersonating workers, thirty-six of these became the first group of non-Beijing students to enter the capital.

April 22 (Saturday)

The *ad hoc* Action Committee, formed by nineteen Beijing universities, had organized a march to Tiananmen Square to take part in Hu's funeral. By the early hours of the 22nd, 200,000 students and citizens were collected together. The committee made three demands: the safety of the students, permission to attend the funeral, and a true report of the police violence on the 20th. After negotiations, the authorities agreed to the first request. At 10:00 a.m. the funeral service began, undisturbed. The funeral service was conducted by Yang Shangkun, and the eulogy was delivered by Zhao Ziyang. After the service three student representatives outside the east wing of the Great Hall tried to present a petition to Li Peng, but were refused. Two of them knelt down, but the other student, Wuer Kaixi, refused to do so.

Students in Xian demonstrated outside the municipal buildings. Some hooligans, mixed among the students, tried to break into the government building, and set fire to it. More than thirty students and a hundred security police were injured.

In Changsha hooligans began looting shops and wrecking cars. Security police arrested nearly a hundred people, none of whom were students.

April 23 (Sunday)

Students from cities around the country arrived continuously in the capital. Student Unions of the Beijing universities formed the Temporary Students' Union of Beijing Universities.

Zhao Ziyang left the country on an official visit to Pyongyang.

April 24 (Monday)

In protest against the attack on students by security officers and the censorship imposed by the government, thirty-five Beijing universities started a strike. Then, breaking forty years of news control, Beijing's *Technology Daily* gave a true report of the students' Movement.

Lists of the relatives of high-ranking officials of the Central Committee appeared on the campuses of Beijing and Qinghua Universities, with demands that the government publicize their financial status and investigate official profiteering and corruption.

April 25 (Tuesday)

A government attempt to communicate with the students through the official National Federation of Students (NFS) failed due to student protests. Over 100,000 students flooded the streets to publicize the goal of their Movement.

Shanghai's *World Economic Herald* published an article quoting speakers at a conference who stated that Hu Yaobang should not have been removed from his post in 1987. Its editor, Yin Banli, resisted orders from Jiang Zemin[7] not to publish. An open letter, signed by 159 teachers from People's University, accused the media of distorting the image of the students.

The Temporary Students' Union organised a "Ten letters per person campaign" to break through the news blockade and report the situation in Beijing to the country, and thereby gain mass support.

April 26 (Wednesday)

An editorial entitled, "The Banner against Turmoil must be raised," appeared in the *People's Daily*. It claimed that the Student Movement had been instigated by a handful of troublemakers in illegal university organizations, that it was a planned conspiracy, a riot and a severe political struggle.

The 38th battalion, 20,000-strong and regarded as the elite of the military, was ordered into the capital.

The Temporary Students' Union held its first press conference. It presented the three demands: (1) equal dialogue with the government, (2) the government should apologize for the Xinhuamen incident, and (3) the New China News Agency and other agencies should report the Student Movement truthfully. The Union stressed that its goals were simply democracy, freedom, science, human rights and the rule by law; and that the means of achieving them would be legal and non-violent. In protest of the April 26th editorial, a large march was to be held the next day.

Beijing's Public Security Office issued an order forbidding any unlicensed demonstrations or marches.

The student representatives of Qinghua University decided to withdraw from the Temporary Students' Union, suggesting the resumption of classes. It also decided not to take part in the next day's demonstration, claiming that "this would scare away the moderate factions" and lead to bloodshed. This decision led to a heated debate and some students accused the leaders of being too meek.

April 27 (Thursday)

The demonstration began at 8:00 a.m. Over 200,000 students took part, and they were cheered on their way by over a million citizens. The students managed to break through eighteen barricades formed by police, with both sides showing restraint, with students even shaking hands with some of the officers caught up in the crowd. Students acted as marshals to prevent trouble-makers from getting mixed among the students. The march lasted fourteen hours.

A spokesman for the State Council, Yuan Mu, made a speech in the afternoon saying that: (1) the government had always welcomed dialogue with the students, (2) students must resume their classes so that the dialogue could be carried out through normal procedures, in a rational and calm manner, (3) the State Council had entrusted the NFS and Beijing Federation of Students (BFS) with the task of arranging the dialogue.

In Hong Kong and Taiwan students declared their support for the Movement in China.

The editor of Shanghai's *World Economic Herald*, Yin Banli, was removed from his post, leading to protests from workers at the newspaper.

April 28 (Friday)

The Autonomous Students' Union of Beijing Universities (ASUBU) was formally established in place of the Temporary Union, with the Beijing Normal University student, Wuer Kaixi, elected as the chairperson and one of the seven Standing Committee members. Wuer Kaixi said that the ASUBU would co-exist with the official organization, the NFS, whose Secretary declared that the government had expressed its wish for a dialogue. On the other hand, the latter had labelled ASUBU as illegal, and the authorities accused some of the student representatives of crimes which might lead them to being arrested at any time.

Representing ASUBU, Wuer Kaixi demanded:
1) that any dialogue must be reported by official news agencies;
2) that there would be no reprisals against student leaders; and
3) that the Student Movement be fairly evaluated.

He also listed the seven purposes of discussion as:

1) to confirm the achievement of Hu Yaobang in the fields of democracy and freedom;
2) to reject the "anti-bourgeois liberalization campaign;"
3) to publicise the financial holdings of high-ranking officials and their families;
4) to create freedom of the press;
5) to increase the budget for education and improve the circumstances of intellectuals;
6) to relax its controls over travel; and
7) to give a true report on the current Student Movement.

In Tianjin a demonstration was held in which over 6000 students took part.

April 29 (Saturday)

Invited by the NFS and BFS, government officials, including Yuan Mu, held discussions with forty-five students from sixteen Beijing universities, which were broadcast live. Wuer Kaixi was invited, but had been instructed beforehand that he would not be allowed to speak. He therefore refused to attend. He told reporters that it was no "dialogue," only an imaginary harmony presented by the government to confuse the students.

Zhao Ziyang returned to China from Pyongyang. It was believed that his absence was the reason for the Politburo's delay in making the final decision with regard to the Student Movement.

April 30 (Sunday)

Because of the firm attitude of Yin Banli and the resistance of his newspaper, the Shanghai Municipal Committee decided to enforce "strict discipline" on the *World Economic Herald* and assign a "working group" to it. This led to heated protest from press and intellectual circles, and also the demand for a dialogue by 150 journalists of the *People's Daily*.

Twenty-nine students from Beijing universities were invited to a discussion with government officials, including the mayor of Beijing, Chen Xitong, on the issue of "official profiteering."

The Central Arts Academy held an exhibition of photographs on the Student Movement. There were over 250 photographs. Some showing the police beating up the students at Xinhuamen were withheld by the authorities.

As rumours of impending secret arrests spread, student leaders of ASUBU temporarily refrained from appearing in public.

May 1 (Monday)

A rally organised by ASUBU in celebration of the May 1st International Labour Day.

May 2 (Tuesday)

Over 10,000 Shanghai students march in protest of the authorities' oppression of the *World Economic Herald,* with order kept by the students' marshals.

May 3 (Wednesday)

At the Youth Rally to Commemorate the Seventieth Anniversary of the May Fourth Movement in Beijing, Zhao Ziyang stated that their demands for an end to corruption and development of education and science were also the wishes of the government. He said that the students must be protected, but stressed that there must be stability as well.

At a press conference, spokesman of the State Council, Yuan Mu, claimed that the Chinese Democracy Alliance in the USA was the "black hand" in control of the Student Movement. He also accused the dissident intellectual, Fang Lizhi, of interference for suggesting that human rights be made a condition of foreign investment.

May 4 (Thursday)

About 200,000 students marched towards Tiananmen Square from various starting points, cheered on by the people. Many of the slogans cried were directed against Yuan Mu's speech. Later, at the Tiananmen Square rally, representatives from ASUBU stressed that the Student Movement was patriotic and not anti-governmental. They also presented a "New May 4th Declaration," calling for democracy, first in universities, and then gradually in the political system.

Over 500 news reporters and editors participated in the students' march. Their slogans included, "We want to tell the truth," "Do not force us to create rumours," and "The people have the right to know the truth."

In Shanghai over 10,000 students held a march and demanded the lifting of the ban on the *World Economic Herald;* similar marches and demonstrations were held in Nanjing, Hangzhou, Guangzhou, Changsha, Wuhan and Xian.

For many days rallies had been held by Chinese students in the USA, UK, Canada and France.

In a meeting with representatives from the Asian Development Bank, Zhao Ziyang analyzed the internal situation in China, and stated that the students were in support of the CCP and they only hoped that the government would correct its mistakes and improve its work. Zhao also pointed to an inadequate legal system and insufficient openness as reasons why the masses were dissatisfied with the government. Zhao wished to hold discussions with workers, intellectuals, students and members of democratic factions, to exchange opinions and solve problems with which they were mutually concerned.

An editorial in the *People's Daily,* entitled "Upholding the May Fourth Spirit and promoting Reform and Modernization," made a milder criticism of the Student Movement, claiming that young people were the new blood during this historic moment of social change. This editorial presented a stark contrast with the ferocious one of April 26th.

May 5 (Friday)

Except for Beijing University and Beijing Normal University, universities in the capital resumed lessons.

ASUBU elected a representative group for the purpose of dialogue with the government.

May 6 (Saturday)

The five representatives from ASUBU's dialogue group submitted a petition to the Office of the Standing Committee of the NPC and the State Council, asking them to send representatives to prepare an open and public dialogue with them.

May 7 (Sunday)

The Central Committee of the CCP told the ASUBU dialogue group to wait one more day for an answer from the government.

May 8 (Monday)

The Government still could not decide on a dialogue with the students. Its Communications Department told the student representatives that the Government would reply before May 11th.

May 9 (Tuesday)

About 1000 editors and news reporters signed and submitted a petition to the Secretariat of the National Union of Journalists requesting a dialogue with the official responsible for monitoring the propaganda work.

May 10 (Wednesday)

Thousands of students marched in support of the fight for freedom of the press.

May 11 (Thursday)

The University students in Beijing decided on a large demonstration to coincide with the visit of Soviet leader, Mikhail Gorbachev, to Beijing on May 15th. They made this decision in protest against the delay in the government's response to their demand for dialogue.

May 12 (Friday)

An editorial in the *People's Daily* by State Council representative, Yuan Mu, emphasised the importance of maintaining a stable environment in China.

May 13 (Saturday)

Some 3000 students started a hunger strike in Tiananmen Square. They demanded the Government start discussions with the students, and that the process be broadcast live on television.

May 14 (Sunday)

The hunger strike entered its second day. Chairman of the Education Commission, Li Tieying, and Beijing Mayor, Chen Xitong, came to visit the students in Tiananmen Square and promised to have a dialogue with them. Secretary of the Central Committee, Yan Mingfu, and Chairman of the Education Commission, Li Tieyin (both Politburo members) spoke with about 30 representatives from ASUBU, including Wuer Kaixi and Wang Dan. However, no agreement was reached.

May 15 (Monday)

More than 130 hunger strikers had been hospitalized, and 800,000 visited the Square to support the students. (In Hong Kong, some twenty students started a hunger strike outside the building of the New China News Agency.)

The talks with Li Tieying and Yan Mingfu continued. Gorbachev was welcomed at Beijing airport by President Yang Shangkun.

May 16 (Tuesday)

The hunger strike entered its fourth day. Over 600 of the 3000 students taking part had been sent to casualty centres. Ten students from the Central Drama Academy decided to stop taking liquids also. University teachers, secondary school students and teachers, editors, journalists and workers marched to support the students in the Square.

Yan Mingfu went to the Square alone and told the students that he had already submitted their requests to the highest level of the government. He asked them to give the government time and to regain their own health.

Zhao Ziyang, while meeting Gorbachev, disclosed that it had been decided at the First Plenary Session of the 13th Central Committee of the CCP that, on most important issues, Deng Xiaoping's guidance was needed.

Student Movements in cities across China demonstrated in support of the Beijing students.

May 17 (Wednesday)

At 2:00 a.m. Zhao Ziyang, representing the Politburo's Standing Committee, presented a written statement to the students acknowledging their patriotism and promising that there would be no reprisals. He hoped that the students would remain calm, rational, restrained, orderly and considerate, and that they would call off the hunger strike.

Over two million people marched to voice their support for the students. Among them were workers, farmers, intellectuals, members of the press, party workers and over 1000 soldiers of the People's Liberation Army.

May 18 (Thursday)

Four Politburo Standing Committee members, Zhao Ziyang, Li Peng, Qiao Shi and Hu Qili, visited some hunger strikers in hospital. These students stated that they were not trying to overthrow the government, that they only wanted to speed up political reforms and revive the people's confidence.

From 11:00 a.m. to noon Premier Li Peng, together with Yan Mingfu and Li Tieying, met with the representatives of ASUBU, including Wuer Kaixi and Wang Dan. Li Peng made it clear that the issue at hand was how to aid the students who were on hunger strike. Wuer Kaixi interrupted Li's speech and asked for more practical discussions. Wang Dan reiterated the demands of the students: (1) that the government reject the April 26th editorial and confirm that the Student Movement is patriotic and not riotous, and (2) broadcast the dialogue.

Li Peng pointed out that the Movement had caused confusion and disorder which had spread throughout the country. He did not answer the students' questions and the meeting ended inconclusively.

This was the sixth day of the hunger strike. Over 2000 people had been hospitalized. About two million people from different occupations had marched in support of the students. Some officers from the PLA sent an open letter to the Central Military Commission in support of the students, and the letter was broadcast to the students in the Square.

May 19 (Friday)

Zhao Ziyang and Li Peng went to Tiananmen Square for the first time to visit the students. With trembling hands and tears in his eyes, Zhao apologised to the students, asking them to call off the hunger strike, saying that such complex issues needed to be solved systematically. Li Peng did not make any speech. At 9:00 p.m. the students ended their hunger strike, replacing it with a sit-in.

Reports stated that, in a Politburo meeting, Zhao proposed a rejection of the April 26th editorial and a concerted attempt at stamping out official profiteering, starting with Deng and his son. Deng was said to be infuriated and said that whoever opposed the editorial destroyed party unity. Later, when the question was put to the vote, sixteen voted for labelling the Movement a riot, with only two voting against. Zhao is said to have handed in his resignation later that night.

Workers in Beijing formed the Beijing Workers' Autonomous Federation (BWAF) in support of the students.

May 20 (Saturday)

A meeting was called by the CCP Central Committee for leading party, military, and government personnel. Li Peng labelled the Student Movement a "riot," and claimed that a handful of people were using it to achieve their political goals. National leader and vice-chairman of the CCP Central Military Commission, Yang Shangkun, spoke immediately after, expressing support for Li's speech and announcing the arrival of the PLA into Beijing to restore order. He stressed that the PLA would not be used against the students. Zhao Ziyang was not seen.

In Tiananmen Square, after listening to a report of Li Peng's speech, students who had called off their hunger strike decided to resume it, and to call on the 200,000 students in the Square to join in. Li Peng declared that from 10:00 a.m. martial law was to be imposed on parts of Beijing. No marches, petitions or strikes were allowed, and censorship of the news was also imposed. Large numbers of troops, along with armoured cars and tanks, marched towards Tiananmen Square. Great numbers of people crowded in the streets and used their own bodies, buses and lorries to barricade the roads, trying to stop the trucks of the PLA from entering the city. It was reported that the soldiers ordered into the city did not know their mission, that for the past week they had not been allowed to read a newspaper, watch television or listen to the radio, and were made to read the April 26th editorial. The TV and radio stations were taken over by troops.

The hunger strike had reached its seventh day. When they learned of the PLA entering the city, student leaders called off the hunger strike. The BWAF called a general strike until the troops were ordered out. ASUBU's dialogue group sent a telegram to Chairman of the NPC, Wan Li, who was on an official visit to Canada, asking him to return and call a meeting of the Standing Committee of the NPC. They said that they would appeal to the law, through the Procurator's Office, against anyone who used violence against the unarmed students; and would also appeal to international human rights groups.

The Beijing masses from all walks of life marched towards Tiananmen Square, disregarding the martial law.

May 21 (Sunday)

Seven senior members of the military[8] sent a letter to the PLA's command centre in the capital and to the Chairman of the CCP Central Military Commission, Deng Xiaoping, requesting that the soldiers not be sent into Beijing. Before dawn, over one million had gathered at the Tiananmen Square. They set up barricades on all the important routes. In addition, more than 20,000 non-Beijing students and workers organized themselves into suicide squads to protect the students in the Square.

Satellite broadcasting from Beijing by foreign television stations was cut at 11:00 a.m. Twelve cities in China saw demonstrations, including Beijing, Xian, Nanjing, Shanghai, Guangzhou and Chengdu. At the same time Chinese and non-Chinese demonstrated in the U.S.A., Canada, Australia, Denmark, Sweden, France, the U.S.S.R. and Japan. About a million students and citizens went on a march along the main roads of Hong Kong Island in support of the Democratic Movement.

May 22 (Monday)

Each province was required to make clear its support for Li Peng's speech before noon. At 10:30 p.m. a clash between the army and the students was reported. Soldiers hit students with belts and bricks. The government denied rumours that it was using force to crackdown.

Wuer Kaixi was removed from ASUBU's Standing Committee after he had urged all the students to retreat from the Square. He fainted after his statement, which was condemned by many students. He believed that the PLA would soon come, and to avoid injuries and death students should leave the Square. At 6:00 p.m. 200,000 students and teachers swore that they would stay there even under the threat of death.

May 23 (Tuesday)

Three persons who had defaced the portrait of Mao Zedong which hangs over the Tiananmen reviewing stand were caught by students and handed over to the police. They identified themselves as a reporter, a teacher and a worker — from Hunan, as their dialect clearly showed. Some forty members of the NPC's Standing Committee had signed a demand for a special meeting of that body — leaving some thirty more required to enforce the request.

May 24 (Wednesday)

The non-Beijing members of the CCP Central Committee appeared in Beijing for a plenum of the Committee. Wan Li cut short his trip to the U.S.A. to return to China.

Large numbers of soldiers arrived in Beijing. Those armies which had earlier retreated from Beijing were stationed in the countryside near the city. Six (of seven) military regions had given support for Li

Peng, as had the PLA's national headquarters. The Beijing Military Region was the only one which had not come out in support.

The satellite link, which had been resumed on 23rd May, 1989, was cut again at 5:00 p.m.

600,000 joined in the Guangzhou-Hong Kong-Macau March that took place in Guangzhou.

May 25 (Thursday)

The students' Main Command Centre for Defending the Tiananmen Square called more than 300 representatives of all the universities in the Square to a meeting. The meeting continued from the afternoon through to the morning of the 26th.

Wan Li's plane landed in Shanghai instead of Beijing.

Li Peng appeared for the first time since his May 20th speech when he met the new ambassadors from Nigeria, Mexico and Burma. He remarked that the present disorders in China would be handled by the Government. He also claimed that Deng Xiaoping was the one who would lead China to the road of reformation and openness, and him alone.

The intellectuals and the BWAF march was joined by students and the press. There were about a million marchers.

Demonstrations and marches in support of the Beijing students were held in cities across China.

May 26 (Friday)

After a democratic vote, the meeting of university representatives adopted the policy that students should stay in the Square, at the same time proposing marches and a hunger strike on an even larger scale, and calling upon the workers to go on strike.

Peng Zhen, former Chairman of the NPC, invited the leaders of democratic parties to a talk in which he emphasized that the government's actions were lawful and constitutional. He also affirmed that what was happening in Beijing was a riot.

The Standing Committee of the CCP Advisory Commission expressed their firm support for Li Peng and Yang Shangkun's speeches of May 20th.

The Beijing Military Region finally gave its support to Li Peng.

May 27 (Saturday)

After a meeting between representatives of student organizations, the BWAF and the Autonomous Union of Citizens, it was decided that a retreat from the Square would take place on May 30th. Meanwhile Wan Li made a statement of support for the May 20th speeches of Li Peng and Yang Shangkun, calling a meeting of the NPC Standing Committee for June 20th. The Chairman of the CPPCC,[9] Li Xiannian, expressed support of Li and Yang.

A twelve-hour concert in Hong Kong raised $12 millions for the students in Beijing.

May 28 (Sunday)

About 1,500,000 people participated in a pro-Movement demonstration in Hong Kong, including members of trade unions and newspapers that usually supported the PRC.

May 29 (Monday)

As there were differences in opinion between the association of Beijing students and those of students from outside Beijing, the work of the Chief Command Centre became difficult. The commander, Chai Ling, and four other Standing Committee members, including Wang Dan, offered their resignation.

The students decided to delay their retreat until June 20th, when the meeting of NPC's Standing Committee was to begin.

The Autonomous Union of Shanghai Universities called on the Shanghai students to "empty the schools" until the beginning of the next school year in September.

May 30 (Tuesday)

The sculpture, Goddess of Democracy, reached Tiananmen Square before dawn and attracted thousands of citizens to the Square.

Leaders of the BWAF were arrested by the public security police. Eleven members of the motorcycle team who had brought news and information to the students were taken into custody.

May 31 (Wednesday)

The *People's Daily* condemned the Goddess of Democracy. At about 10:00 a.m. a man tried to push down the sculpture but was stopped by the students. In the face of increasing disorder, the Chief Command Centre appointed Gua Haifang to be the commander responsible for restoring order.

To the south of Beijing ordinary people marched shouting slogans in support of the government, and burned a facsimile of Fang Lizhi. Their demonstrations were promoted by the government and the CCP.

In the evening about 3000 students demonstrated in Tiananmen Square against the arrest of the workers' leaders. Nearly 10,000 students and workers then marched to the Public Security Office and demanded to know the reasons for the arrests. Later, the union reported that they had been released earlier.

June 1 (Thursday)

Student leaders Chai Ling and Fang Chunde told reporters that a kidnap attempt had been made against them. They struggled and shouted, causing the kidnappers to run off. Chai Ling claimed that a member of the Standing Committee of the Autonomous Students' Union of non-Beijing Universities, Lien Xiende, was one of the four persons responsible.

The *People's Daily* had a long article on Hu Yaobang. It gave credit to Hu for rehabilitating thousands of officials and intellectuals persecuted during the Cultural Revolution.

Several big hotels in Beijing hung slogans on their exteriors supporting the Government.

ASUBU reorganized its Standing Committee. Wuer Kaixi and Wang Dan were no longer members.

June 2 (Friday)

More than 200,000 soldiers had already been stationed around Beijing. The military had taken over control of all the communications. Before dawn about 10,000 soldiers were given orders to march toward the Tiananmen Square along Changan Avenue. However, they were blocked by thousands of citizens and students near the Beijing Hotel, and the army retreated.

As the day began, a police car with no plates raced through the Fuxingmen intersection, mounted the sidewalk and knocked down four people — two of whom died instantly. An eye-witness remarked that before this incident several jeeps had already driven through at high speed. The two policemen responsible were taken away after a few minutes by another police car. The injured were raced to hospital by nearby citizens. Several thousand people were angered by this irresponsibility and marched spontaneously towards Tiananmen Square.

The Beijing Municipal Government again organized peasants into marches. They shouted slogans in support of the government. One of the marchers said that each of them were given money, a straw hat and a two-day holiday.

About a thousand Beijing students demonstrated shouting sarcastic slogans like, "Support authoritarianism," "Support dictatorial rule," "Support Li Peng." When they marched along Changan Avenue, a large number of citizens watched, and when they realized that the students were being satirical, they cheered and applauded.

Popular songwriter, Hou Dejian, Beijing University lecturer, Liu Xiao, head of the planning department of Stone Computer Corporation, Zhou Duo, and the CCP member, Gao Xin, started their 72-hour hunger strike in Tiananmen Square at 4:00 p.m.

June 3-4 (Saturday-Sunday)

In the early hours of June 3rd, crowds blocked military trucks at Jianguomen and Xidan. Inside the trucks they found machine guns, rifles, gas masks, etc., which they took to exhibit at Xinhuamen, attracting 10,000 onlookers.

During the course of the day (as in the previous few days), military-looking people, dressed in civilian clothes, were seen in the city familiarising themselves with the layout.

At noon about 2000 soldiers and military police with iron helmets and clubs, came out from the west gate of the Zhongnanhai Compound trying to disperse the crowds in Xidan Avenue and at Xinhuamen. The police broadcast warnings, fired tear-gas, and dispersed the crowd with violence. Meanwhile, about 300 soldiers suddenly dashed out of Xinhuamen, waving their clubs and cattle prods, beating up whoever they laid their eyes on. Students of the Political-Legal University who had been sitting-in there for two weeks were forced to leave. At Xidan soldiers dispersed the crowd with rubber bullets, wounding many.

At about 2:00 p.m. over 10,000 military police rushed out from the west gate of the Great Hall of the People to form a blockade; but the crowd blocked them with two buses. After futile discussions between students and soldiers, with casualties on both sides, all of the troops withdrew. Over 100,000 people were gathered on Changan Avenue. They angrily overturned a jeep that was parked on the road side and smashed the windshields of two military vehicles. From the early hours to the evening of June 3rd, numerous clashes broke out between civilians and military, both sides increasingly emotional.

After 6:00 p.m. the government broadcast three warnings in the media, indicating that violent suppression was imminent. The first one was issued at 6:00 p.m., saying that "martial law troops, public security officers and military police have the right to deal forcefully with anyone who does not take heed of the warning and violates the martial law." The second warning was at 8:30 p.m., repeating that the troops were to use all necessary means to remove opposition. Meanwhile there were tens of thousands of people in the Square, including students, workers and civilians. The third warning was issued at 10:00 p.m., cautioning people to stay indoors or risk danger. In the meantime, the atmosphere was tense in the Square.

At 11:00 p.m. gunshots were heard at Muxidi, signifying that troops were advancing onto the Square. Shortly after midnight two armoured cars moved along Changan from the west, driving aside all obstacles, clearly making way for military vehicles to follow.

At 1:25 a.m. about 600 soldiers advanced towards the Great Hall of the People shooting into the air. They were about 100 metres away from the crowd.

At 1:40 a.m. the soldiers arrived at the Great Hall of the People. At 2:00 a.m. Changan was alive with gunshots, and soldiers of the 27th Group Army surrounded the Square. At 4:00 a.m. the "clean-up" started. The lights in the Square flashed on and off. The noise of gunfire mingled with the cries of the victims, the hysterical laughter of the slaughterers, and the rumble of tanks. After a short time ambulance sirens were added to the noise. At daybreak there was a pile of bodies covered by canvas in the Square.

For the next few days tanks lined the Square, the soldiers busied themselves cleaning the ground and burning lifeless objects, and afterwards helicopters took the remains away in sacks.

The 27th Army continued its mission of suppressing the "counter-revolutionary riot." Rifle shots were heard wherever they went. Among the "counter-revolutionary hooligans" were a nine year-old boy and a three year-old girl. One hospital reported that the oldest victim was over seventy, while the youngest was thirteen.

Aftermath

By June 5th, over 5000 had died, and 30,000 had been injured. On June 6th, the suggestion that of 7000 were killed was being heard, not to mention the "missing." The bodies of those who had died in the early hours of June 4th would never be recovered. On June 7th, Yuan Mu, spokesman for the State Council, stated that, in the oppression of the anti-revolutionary riot, 5000 soldiers of the People's Liberation Army and 2000 civilians were injured, while the death toll amounted to less than 400, including only twenty-three students. The government declared ASUBU and BWAF to be illegal organizations, and ordered their leaders to give themselves up or be regarded as criminals. A hotline was also set up for informers to call and turn in those who had been active in the Movement.

On June 9th, Deng Xiaoping appeared on television for the first time since May 16th, congratulating the martial law troops. Accompanying Deng were Li Peng, Yang Shangkun, Peng Zhen, Wan Li, Li Xiannian, Qiao Shi and Yao Yilin; but Zhao Ziyang and Hu Qili were not seen. He said of those taking part in the Movement, "Their aim was to topple the Communist Party, socialism and the entire People's Republic of China, and set up a capitalist republic." About the army, he said, "They are truly the people's army, China's Great Wall of steel. They have stood and passed this test." He did not mention the civilians and students who were killed, ending with, "The direction established by the party at the 3rd Plenum [1978] was correct, as was the adoption of the Four Cardinal Principles — both are correct!"

NOTES

1. This chronology was provided by Mok Chiu Yu and the "Hong Kong Group" organized to promote the true story of events in the Square through publication of underground documents from the PRC.

2. Pasting up a "character poster" in a public place is an established mode of political comment in Chinese society, especially where that comment is critical of the regime which controls all other media forms.

3. Xinhuamen is the main gate to the walled compound for senior government officials (called Zhongnanhai) to the northwest of Tiananmen Square.

4. Born in 1942, Yan was director of the Political Studies Institute of the Chinese Academy of Social Sciences, and a government adviser. He is now in exile in France.

5. Born in 1937, Bao was research fellow at the Institute of Chinese History of the Chinese Academy of Social Sciences.

6. A reporter on the newspaper, *Guangming Daily*.

7. Politburo member and Shanghai party boss who was later to replace Zhao Ziyang after the latter had been purged.

8. These were PLA navy commander Ye Fei, former Minister of Defence Zhang Aiping, former deputy Minister of Defence Xiao Ke, former chief of the PLA general staff Yang Dezhi, Korean War hero and former President of the PLA military academy Song Shilun, former PLA commander Chen Zaidao, and former politcal commissar of the PLA logistics department Li Jukui.

9. The Chinese People's Political Consultative Conference, established in 1949, legitimised the creation of the PRC. Later eclipsed by the National People's Congress, it remains operative as an organ for the organization and administration of various non-communist parties and groups, whose activities complement, and are guided by, CCP policy.

THEORETICAL ANALYSIS

I: Wang Dan,[1] The Star of Hope Rises in Eastern Europe

More than thirty years ago, Khrushchev's secret report to the CPSU,[2] the Polish and Hungarian events,[3] and our own Hundred Flowers Movement, provided moments of scintillating possibility for an international communist movement hovering on the edge of irrelevance. The saddest thing was that each was followed by a long period of military-autocratic rule in those countries. Today, however, eastern Europe is again reminding us of the spirit of 1956.

In February, 1989, the Hungarian Socialist Workers' Party [the ruling communist party] recognised the 1956 events as a "genuine people's uprising." The Hungarian party congress affirmed a multiparty system and pluralism, with the formation even of a "non-party faction."

Face-to-face meetings in Poland have produced concrete results, with opposition organizations like Solidarity and the Writers' Union, having been legalised, organising massive demonstrations. On February 10th, Premier Jaruzelski declared that the Polish United Workers' Party would be "giving up its monopoly of power."

· In Czechoslovakia, in spite of the caution and indecisiveness of the regime, there have been frequent and decisive actions by the masses. Recently, over one thousand cultural workers petitioned Premier Strougal to demand the release of students arrested in the Prague demonstrations in January.

What is happening in eastern Europe should teach us two things. First, we see that the dictatorship of one party (or some similar system known by a different name) should be abandoned, the introduction of democratic politics being a major trend in socialist development. It is now obvious that a refusal to reform the political system is an attempt to protect vested interests, and is against the tide of change. Second, the promising developments in those countries must be attributed to the ceaseless efforts of the opposition inside both the party and the general population. Their prolonged and untiring efforts in pursuit of freedom of speech and the protection of human rights is responsible for the creation of a healthy political atmosphere. It also reaffirms that democracy is not a gift, but the product of struggle from below by the people themselves. In this struggle, the educated elite must play a leading role by acting as a vanguard.

We think that the path taken by Poland, Hungary and Czechoslovakia is the only way to save socialist countries from their internal crises. Political developments in China must learn from these countries. Let us bluntly state: Only when China follows in the footsteps of these eastern European countries, and only then, will full democracy and full development be successfully accomplished.

March 4, 1989

II: *Wang Dan, On Freedom of Speech for the Opposition*

Although freedom of speech is proclaimed as an important principle in the Chinese Constitution, it has clearly been violated in an authoritarian manner. This is shown by the illegal and violent suppression of opposition voices by the political authorities. That suppression is based upon the formula that, Truth equals the World View of the Proletariat, which is equated with Marxism, which is equated with the World View of the CCP, which is equated with the proclamations of the Party Organs, which is equated with the views of the Leadership. There is no need even to comment further upon such poor logic.

Possible reasons for restricting freedom of speech are,

1) the ruling party knows the truth and properly represents the interests of the people,
2) the party has a responsibility to protect the people from the erroneous and practically dangerous views of an opposition, and
3) the growth of the opposition will disturb the prosperity, unity, and normal path of development of society.

To counter the first argument we can argue as follows:

a) There is no absolute truth, and truth is not held by a monopoly. Certainly the proletariat may grasp it, as may capitalists, as may a minority. Hence the statement, "everyone is equal before the truth." Even if the opposition's views are obviously flawed, it cannot be said with certainty that there is no element of truth in their ideas. Truth ought not be suffocated and weakened by its monopolization.

b) Those who know truth will not suppress opposition. On the contrary, fallacious argument leads to the promotion of truth through unfavorable comparison with the latter. Without this confrontation, that which is true loses its strength. Therefore, the suppression of opposition is a sign of weakness and lack of confidence, obstructing the promotion of that which is true.

c) People are diverse, and every stratum in society has its own special interest. The ruling party cannot represent everyone, at best representing the majority; and even then the legitimate interest of any individual citizen ought not be dismissed, but promoted through legitimate channels. Who can be so certain that the views of an opposition do not represent the legitimate interests of some small group of people? However, in such a situation, it might also be the case that the demands of the majority are being suppressed.

d) Political parties are made up of a whole range of individuals, including those who want to use power to satisfy their greed and ambition, and do so by distorting truth and fooling the masses. Without critical voices those consumed by ambition could fearlessly pursue their ends by distortion of the truth. Even if the party had a supervisory mechanism, it would be ineffective if it came under the control of such people. Moreover, China is in fact a political system monopolised by one party, and no effective mechanism of control can develop within it. Therefore, suppression of the views of the opposition encourages the corrupt elements who have infiltrated the party, which become the greatest danger to the party's ability to govern. Such is particularly true of our autocracy, where we see the suppression of opposition linked with the distortion of truth.

e) It should be permissible to criticise that which is true. We should remember that truth does not merely concern grand theories of human development. Truth involves such simple and self-evident statements as, "a sated person cannot be hungry." If I rushed around saying that we can eat our fill and still be hungry, I would not be punished, although I might be treated as a fool. Why not? Because this kind of opposition to truth is absurd. Therefore, if the views of the opposition generate intellectual confusion, it must be because some elements therein are correct. This must mean, first, that a minority can possess truth; and, second, that, whilst the absurd goes unpunished, the merely erroneous (but which contains *some* truth) is restricted. This is unjust. If communism also has truth, but cannot be criticised, it must be a function of the possession of arbitrary power. And how can things that must depend on arbitrary power be regarded as true?

The following can be used to counter the second argument (i.e., that the CCP must protect the people from erroneous views):

a) By recognising that the government and CCP must prevent deviance under the aegis of "political leadership," you encourage the secret perpetration of such views. The result is that the criticism is hidden, cannot be punished, and continues to influence the people. The suppression of free speech becomes responsible for the perpetration of such errors as may exist in opposition views.

b) As government should represent the will of the citizenry, so should there be mutual trust between the two. Fear of the opposition shows that the government holds the citizens in contempt. Only a government that rejects the slogan that, "the people's eyes are clear and bright," would attempt to suppress criticism.

c) However fallacious the opposition's views they should be permitted; for it is only the censorship authorities who call them erroneous. Now value judgments differ, and censors can never represent the majority of the people. Only when ideas are allowed to circulate freely will it be possible to judge on the question of their truth.

d) Freedom, like personal property,[4] is an inviolable human right. Marx himself likened the freedom of speech, association and assembly to "soil, air, light, and space." This is a very apt analogy; for, if thieves, fools and the insane should enjoy this privilege, even the views of an opposition might be allowed to circulate freely.

e) If opposition views create extremely undesirable consequences, the government can easily and legally punish it. However, there is no logic to the policy of prior restraint.

Finally, the third argument (i.e, that an opposition will create instability) can be rejected as follows:

Political activity generates many contradictions in practice, and these must be seen as balancing each other. If one side possesses a domineering coercive capacity, then imbalance will occur, creating social turmoil. For forty years we have suppressed opposition views, and still there is no unity and stability. On the contrary, we had ten years of turmoil [during the Great Proletarian Cultural Revolution, 1966-1976]. We must conclude that democratic politics will only occur when opposition views can circulate and opposition parties are permitted. Only then will the normal order of political life in society be properly maintained. Suppression of free speech will, by contrast, generate turmoil.

Please note that we do not support total freedom of speech. There must always be self-control; and absolute freedom is impossible. However, we do object to external restraints, especially those imposed upon us by violent means.

In this new Chinese enlightenment the intellectuals must make freedom of speech the priority. They must have the courage to criticise injustice, including the decisions of party and government officials. As intellectuals, we can influence others only with ideas and words. If freedom of speech is lost, intellectuals will not be able to promote the democratization process, we will lose our independent position, and we will become adjuncts of the party and government — as we have been for the past forty years!

[undated]

*III: Ren Wanding,[5] Why Did the Rally In Memory of Hu Yaobang
Turn Into a Democracy Movement?*

Since April 15th, Beijing has seen the emergence of a huge
Democracy Movement, with participants as numerous as those involved in the April Fifth Movement of 1976.

In fact, the death of the former General Secretary of the CCP
should not have been commemorated in such an excessive manner.
Like the April Fifth incident [in 1976], people took the opportunity to
commemorate a dead man in order to wage an anti-feudal, anti-
authoritarian, pro-socialist struggle. However, we must also remember that, at the time of the Democracy Wall Movement of 1979,
when Hu Yaobang advised that, "people should not be arrested," the
main leaders were arrested and prosecuted. At the present time the
people's emotions, thoughts and ideas have been directed towards a
criticism of the entire structure of the socio-political system of China.
How should one respond to this?

There has never been any simple way of interpreting history;
nor can any power define the character of historical truth. The CCP
co-opted the slogans of the Democracy Wall Movement, and conditions improved for the people. Nevertheless, the evil suffered by
forty years of monolithic party rule gave rise to numerous com-
plaints.

Inevitably there appeared such shocking demands as, "Overthrow the Autocracy," and "Down with Dictatorship," in Tiananmen
Square. The New China News Agency stated in its April 26th editorial that people were shouting the slogan, "Down with the Communist Party!" Slogans like, "Long Live Democracy, Human Rights, and
Freedom," became loud and frequent in the protest Movement. The
Internationale was sung again and again, with new meaning and significance.

No reasonable observer would attribute these developments to the ulterior motives of a small number of disruptive
agitators. Those who use this interpretation are trying to protect their privileges, and the people will not accept such lies. In
1986 people were wrongly sent to jail for initiating student and
worker demonstrations. I would like the legal authorities to
open up their files.

Meanwhile, if the party cannot handle this Movement of the people, then the party must soon disappear. The workers will develop consciousness and link hands with the students.

Chinese politics is a huge reflection of the "eight-in-one" principle: party and power as one, party and government as one, party and legal system as one, party and State as one, party and the armed forces as one, party and people as one, party and the economy as one, and party and culture as one.

The Constitution merely defines the territory within which civil rights can be exercised, with specific limits. The rights of the government prevail over those of private individuals. The law is clearly restrictive and repressive, not open and expansive, on matters of civil rights.[6]

The existing and proposed regulations concerning demonstrations will, in a country where there is no rule of law, like China, necessarily become the chains that increase control and reduce the actuality of civil rights.

The Communist Party has in the past initiated a Cultural Revolution and many other ideological campaigns in violation of constitutional norms. The civil rights of more than a billion people have been denied for a long time. Several million people who were in social reform movements, party and non-party members, were persecuted and/or executed. That is the CCP's unforgivable crime against the Chinese people.

That the Chinese communists have ignored the loud call, from here and from beyond the borders of China, for the amnesty and release of those imprisoned for participation in the Democracy Wall Movement, again reveals the painful fact that, in a totalitarian one-party system, where there can be no rule of law, the law itself can be used as a brutal instrument for the repression of political opposition. The party remains above the law and can ignore the Constitution.

Public opinion at home and abroad calls for the release of certain political prisoners. How could this affect the stability of the country?

Examine the turmoils in modern China. Which one has not been caused by internal conflicts in the CCP? If there were no conflicts in the party, the country would have been saved from disruption.

The appearance here of harmony, stability and unity is grounded in the bloody repression of the masses, and in the bloody incarceration and execution of millions of the finest people in our country. We do not need that kind of false harmony and solidarity, brought on not by the wishes of the people, but brought on by the selfish goals of the one party and its eight subordinate systems of control.

To be sorry after having hit your children, the people; and to ask us to forgive the ugliness of our mother, the party; such are the excuses of those with the mentality of gangsters. No matter what the Constitution says, it will be necessary for us to continue to fight for our rights. Many members of both the CCP and democratic movements have lost their lives; but we must still try to ensure that the Constitution is untainted by those cliques of selfish profiteers, with their decadence, corruption and coercion.

Human rights are the rights of the people, and can exist only in a democracy, as an intrinsic part of democracy. The Enlightenment and social progress in Europe had their revolutionary beginnings in the respect for human rights and the individual.

We must strongly object to the accusation that we are using legal arguments as a basis for illegal actions, and to the suppression of our legal activities. Actions cannot be legal and illegal at the same time. If our actions are permitted in law, then they are legal.

On the other hand, constitutional reform is required, and the people's Movement is appealing to legal experts. In the Constitution we see defined the rights possessed by the people of China. However, these articles are only high-sounding, abstract and empty words. If the Four Cardinal Principles [7] do not disappear, they will always take priority over human rights, and the statement that "power belongs to the people" will be a fraud. If the monolithic socio-political structure is not eliminated, and replaced with a pluralist society and culture, then the "open door" policy and reform will be like a picture of food hanging on a wall — not satisfying. To reform the country's social system was the chief goal of the Democracy Wall Movement ten years ago, and remains so for the Popular Movement now and into the future.

Students! If the monolithic and imperial structure cannot be fundamentally changed, how can education save the country? Does the unity and well-being of the nation depend upon mobilization by a party, or does it depend on the voluntary coming together of individuals who are truly free and vested with rights? The slogan of the May Fourth Movement, necessary at that time [1919], was, "Save the country and struggle to survive." The Democracy Wall Movement performed a similar task, identifying the illusory condition and interests of the country, as defined by our rulers, and stating the real interests. The Democracy Wall Movement also met the needs of the time, represented the essential feelings of the masses, and raised the revolutionary standard of human rights and democracy; and it is that which gave historical significance to it.

However, although the demands for human rights of the Democracy Wall Movement were similar to those of the May Fourth Movement, their significance was different, for they were demands made of a communist government which had been in power since 1949. Thus, democracy and human rights are eternal themes, and we will be demanding them still on the centennial anniversary of the May Fourth Movement, the mantle of the latter inherited by a revolutionary Popular Movement, establishing not a politics of power, but a politics of people's democracy.

The Chinese have arrived at a crucial juncture for popular rights, people's democracy, and social reform. Earlier movements were cruelly repressed, and many of their participants are still in prison. Even those who have been released suffer from discrimination. However, the contradictions remain, with demands for reform threatening the "eight-in-one" system, and the profiteering of party and government officials.

What is the situation? We have greed and corruption, legal distortions, political degeneration, party regulations and discipline ignored, rampant inflation, increasing theft, people furious, people suffering, no firm laws and systemic crisis. In this situation, the earlier reforms look like being abandoned.

In modern China the Democracy Movement has had various forms. Again and again, huge protests and demonstrations informed the communist rulers and forced them to correct their mistakes by charting a new course. At times it looked like turmoil, but what was the alternative for the country and the governing party? What good did simple petitions ever do? So today, the wreaths at the Monument, the masses in Tiananmen Square, the marches along

Changan, and the demonstration outside Xinhuamen, are all appropriate ways of educating the party.

If the Democracy Movement has made a mistake over time, it has been its failure to form its own political parties, not developing beyond a series of popular Movements. It is true that the basis of the PRC is not to be found in the degenerate field of politics and party style, but in the heroism of a series of people's Movements. The people are the true radicals, the truly wise, the least corrupt and most powerful. The increasing incidence of their popular Movements, in this age of communications, indicates that our contemporary, monolithic, imperial order can not last — unless it closes the door on the world.

However, a freely-formed association is a common means for the transformation of society. The full development of the people's Democracy Movement, and its growing sophistication, will inevitably lead to the union of social organizations and leadership into political parties. Recent popular Movements here and in Taiwan have shown the persistence of democratic forces, which in their variety cannot be contained in a single political party.

The Democracy Wall Movement produced a simple programme, the Chinese Declaration of Human Rights, and a loose political organization, the Human Rights League. Various organizations arranged for joint meetings and common declarations for joint activities. The Student Movement in 1986 had only vague slogans for democracy, human rights, and freedom. There was no concrete programme or long term goals, and it did not voice the feelings of the masses concerning economic matters. In both cases, members of the working class associated with the movement were arrested and jailed. The lesson is that our organizations were too small. Students should join with the workers, who in their turn should fight for independent trade unions. Only when several million production workers understand that their democratic rights are not handed down to them, but are something that must be fought for, and take command of the situation, will democracy be realised.

In your dialogue with the government, amnesty for those arrested during the earlier movements must be an important part of the discussion. Further, we must fight for 1) higher wages and oppose inflation; 2) basic housing at low prices; 3) democracy in the universities, and opposition to administrative hierarchy; and 4) freedom of the press to oppose counter-revolutionary thought.

Workers! Brothers! Organise; but legally! Long live the coalition of students and workers!

Speech of April 21, 1989, in Tiananmen Square.

IV: Ren Wanding, Reflections on the Historical Character of the Democracy Movement [8]

Look at Tiananmen Square, the symbol of the rich land of the People's Republic of China! Look at the battlefield of the Xidan Democracy Wall Movement! Look at the Square from which the storm of the May Fourth Movement first began to blow!

The Importance of the Democracy Movement

This is a confrontation between masses of students and thousands of armed policemen and soldiers; but it is also a confrontation between the citizens of Beijing and the government, a political challenge and power struggle by people from all levels of society against the party. The massive demonstration, which began on April 27th, is another masterpiece of the people's Democracy Movement. To combat the authorities' irrational accusation that it created "turmoil," on April 27th the students of Beijing's institutions of higher education, and several hundred thousand ordinary citizens, marched through the city's streets in columns that stretched for miles. They broke through the police and military barriers many times, and gathered successfully in Tiananmen Square in the afternoon. Wherever the marchers went they were welcomed by the people, and given food and money. It became the greatest and most wonderful demonstration in the history of China. Not simply a student movement, it is a great Democracy Movement led by the students and joined by all levels of society.

During the last forty years, when has the people's democratic power been so well demonstrated? When has the authority of the ruling CCP dropped to such a low level? The party finds it impossible to restore its control over the situation and the confidence of the people. The people are not opposed to the CCP's rule, but it has performed so badly that it has lost the sympathy, support and understanding of the people. The party has suppressed democracy. Although it has many extraordinary members, they cannot change its fundamentally flawed political basis, nor its anti-democratic character. I repeat, people are not moving against socialism, but a socialist system led by a party that has performed badly. It has not created greater wealth and democracy, but has placed the burden of inflation on the people in a perpetual exploitation of them.

Over the past ten years of economic reform and an "open door" policy, in spite of some socio-economic progress, there has continued extensive corruption in the economy and the perpetuation of evil features of the political system. The party condemns those who criticise it, when they should be asking themselves why the criticism is there. To criticise the Popular Movement as the "conspiracy of a few people" is to cheat the people, and probably cheat themselves into even bigger political mistakes. The Chinese Communist Party has created a socio-political structure which is monolithic, the "eight-in-one," and which must now leave the historical scene.

The Movement's Historical Position

During the past forty years, beginning in the fifties when the democratic parties[9] tried to obtain equal status with the Communist Party, through the April Fifth revolution of 1976, through the Democracy Wall Movement from '79 to '81, through the student Movements in '85 and '86, through the intellectuals' petition for the release of victims from the Democracy Wall Movement in 1989, up to this Democracy Movement led by the students, we have developed maturity. If we cannot now show that this Movement represents everyone, then we cannot take on responsibility for the future of China.

The truth is that democracy is growing rapidly, developing theories and principles, but pays a high price for the experience it gains. The Democracy Wall Movement made political demands that were more mature than those of the May Fourth Movement, demanding a popular basis for democracy, Marxism and socialism. Moreover, the Democracy Wall Movement was the first to demand a reform of our current monolithic socio-political structure. Its specific arguments replaced the ambiguous poetry of May Fourth, principles replaced slogans, analysis replaced noise, and free societies replaced disorganised groups. Furthermore, this Democracy Movement, initiated by the institutions of higher education, has reached a new level. Its features are: autonomous organizations in each institution, a joint committee for these, joint action, and the full exercise of our rights as defined in the PRC Constitution. The movement has slogans and short-term tactics and goals; but no long-term objectives, fixed rules, firm organization, or support system.

Can the Communist Party be Replaced?

People should realise that the operation of the Popular Movement shows that society requires a new party organization and leadership. The historical circumstances and the will of the people necessitate it. The 1989 Democracy Movement is the embryo of the new party, a new societal organization. Perhaps this infant will die in the cradle, but it will surely be reborn in the next upheaval. My view is that the long-term goal of the movement is to reform, peacefully, the Communist Party's monolithic socio-political structure, and to replace it with a diversified democratic, cultural, national framework. This is the proposed ideal of the young scholars in the social sciences, and this is the right moment to make it happen. If we must get bloodied in the process, let it be so. Force must be met with force. The monolithic feudal structure is the product of a long period of feudalism and low economic output. With economic development and social development, it must now disappear from China. Do the Chinese like and accept totalitarianism and monolithic dictatorship? The current democratic wave denies that. However, if they are disliked by the people, why does the Communist Party force us to accept them? Why does the party think that only it can represent the people, that only it can consolidate the benefits of development? And can the party be replaced? Are we not only already beaten, but also immature weak and stupid, if we are opposing something that we think cannot be replaced? Have millions of brilliant Chinese been killed or imprisoned since 1949 for no reason at all?

Students! The historic burden is now on your shoulders. It is now time to organise a legal party and associations, formally to participate in the reform of the social system of China. The truth is that, though one may have a family and private interests, those who are the intellectual elite of society, whatever their age, must make the effort. Walking out of our institutions, steeled by the heat of the situation, we shall succeed. China does not lack the capacity for democratic politics, but it is suppressed. Countering this suppression, as when we ignored the decree banning demonstrations, we shall succeed.

The CCP Responds to Good Will with Hatred

The short-run objectives of the Movement should be the effective protection of the people's rights as defined by the Constitution, and dispensing with all of the irrational accusation that ours is an "illegal social formation." The legal rights to demonstrate and to strike must prevail over the accusation that we are creating "turmoil." The legal right to freedom of speech must overcome the irrational accusation that we are behaving unconstitutionally and going against CCP leadership. Only if we can counteract these accusations can our Movement continue, and the legality of our actions be recognised.

To destroy the CCP, or to oppose the CCP, are two different things. The first is a criminal act. The latter concerns the conflict between the Four Cardinal Principles and the Constitution of the PRC, which provides the right of free speech. Officials interpret this in any way they want. If the one party cannot be opposed, where is freedom of speech, where is socialist democracy?

Today, the fairest measure of freedom of speech is whether or not the ruling party can be opposed, without which it is only false and abstract propaganda. The monolithic structure of the party is the political and theoretical question. Even if the Movement is not opposed to the party, the intellectuals will be. Wisdom and politics cannot be separated. If the party cannot be opposed, then at times it will be dominated by destructive elements like the Gang of Four, who *are* the party for a time. Further, unopposed, the party can initiate random campaigns, directed against anybody, hurting people, party and country at random, without any understanding of what is being done. There are other so-called democratic parties, but what power do they have? So what value is the "long term co-existence of parties"? The ideological and cruel class struggles of the CCP continue without sign of remorse, which is the consequence of the impossibility of opposing the party. How many have suffered for the maintenance of the party's dictatorship? Only a minority of the population; but the legal and political institutions thereby repress everybody.

How can the party oppose its critics? The popular democracy opposes the *mistakes* of the party, which must benefit the nation and the rights of the people. Where's the problem? The Popular Movement awakens the party, preventing corruption there and in the society. To this good will they respond with hatred? With incarceration and dishonest rectification, the vicious relationship between ruler and ruled is continued in China, with so much suffering.

Since the current social system cannot be opposed, the stagnant economic system persists, threatening the national economy; for, since the social system cannot be opposed, the restrictive economic system, and the serfdom of the rural economy, continues. If the party and the socialist system had accepted opposition ideas, how many evil incidents could have been avoided in the past? And now, by correcting its mistakes, the socialist system could demonstrate its future superiority.

The Evil that Remains

Over the last decade, although there has been a widespread reform of our economic system, and some movement towards an "open-door" policy in international relations, the basic structure of the "eight-in-one" system has not been touched, and some possibilities have not been considered. False prosperity and hidden crises occur; and for the past ten years the party's policy has come to be based on three things:

1) The death of Mao Zedong, and the opportunity thereby for the party to reject his idealistic socialist policies.

2) The gradual policy change following the power struggle of October 1976, consequent upon the April Fifth Movement, without which there could not have been an "October Incident." [10]

3) The Xidan "Democracy Wall Movement," which exploded in 1978, placed a priority on political and economic reform, with particular reference to the ending of life-tenure for those in party and bureaucratic positions. Without Democracy Wall there would not have been the freedom of speech and the new lifestyle that you see around you today.

The party and government should be instruments of the people's will. The Third Plenum of the Eleventh Central Committee [in 1978] produced nothing to that end. Consequently, people associated with the Democracy Wall Movement remain illegally incarcerated to this day. Students, you should show some interest in this shady judicial question, and request their release and rehabilitation. The decade of [economic] reform, and the "open door policy" [in foreign relations and foreign investment] is a case of the government granting some concessions to the people, but maintaining the repression of the intellectual elite.

The method of oppression remains the same. The fact that Hu Yaobang twice spoke against the arbitrary arrest of Democracy Wall activists at a seminar in 1979, proves only that a party leader cannot rescue people, however virtuous and brave he may be. The monolithic "eight-in-one" principle can represent only the will of the party, and never the will of the people. Nor does the State Council, as the popular Movements during the past thirteen years demonstrate. Why do people express their ideas thus? Obviously because the ruling party, the government, the People's Congress, and the State Council do not represent them. The whole charade can be seen in the control of the electorate during elections. The corruption of the party, the politicians, the bureaucrats and the legal system is a tragic fact! Lies cannot cover up the promotion of the Four Cardinal Principles and the "eight-in-one" principle against the welfare of the people. Unless this is changed, when the party goes wrong, everything goes wrong.

How Can the Situation be Changed?

Because the Constitution protects the "eight-in-one" position, we can begin with the amendment of the Constitution. If that document and the State Council are unrepresentative, the way to do this must be through the institutions of higher education. It is necessary to organise People's Committees, based upon the grassroots organization of professors, intellectuals, and people from all levels, which will begin to exercise governmental functions, including the formation of new parties. Through them the theory of democratic politics can be transformed into practice; and they are necessary for this.

Such a change has been envisaged for many years by intellectuals representing the people — unlike in Poland where the same process was led by the trade unions. Such committees were suggested on the Democracy Wall ten years ago. In Poland the Solidarity union held a dialogue with, and worked with, the ruling party, providing us with a precedent. If we do not follow it, a corrupt politics will persist, an unstable China will achieve neither solidarity nor stability, and improved government policy will be impossible.

Our goals become: the creation of political parties, and government by people's committees, each of which have a popular basis. It has been said that, "Politics is the elimination of selfishness, without which justice will perish." China belongs to the Chinese, not to one or more political parties. If the CCP recognises the reality of the situation, it will not be surprised by popular dissatisfaction, and will not make irrational claims and criticisms concerning the relationship of the party to the people.

Viewed from a distance, China reminds us of the seventeenth century. The real foundations of the country should be democracy and liberty, not so many cardinal principles. Divisions within China in recent years were not created by the people. As in every other era when conflicts occurred, it was the evil result of a centralised and feudalistic monopoly of political power. It is now hindering our historical development, and the people must dispense with such false unity. The coercive unity of China, achieved in 1949, should give way to the popular franchise and people's committees. The intellectuals should inspire the people, demanding the return of power to the people. Opposition, hesitation, pessimism, or new authoritarianism are futile. Only the great power of democracy, and a people's organization created by it, can stabilise China and further stimulate its population.

The present and the future belong to the people!

Students, you are the pride of the nation, and I love you for it!

April 27-May 4, 1989

V: Our "April Student Movement" and the "April Fifth Movement" [11]

There are some startling similarities between the April Patriotic-Democratic Student Movement and the April Fifth Movement. We can look at these from many angles, including that of the *People's Daily*, which accuses the two movements of possessing the following similarities:

The April Fifth Movement [of 1976], according to the authorities,

1) was a counter-revolutionary incident;
2) utilised big and small character posters, poetry, essays and cartoons viciously to attack the leadership of the country and the party;
3) was essentially an attempt to overthrow the leadership of the CCP and the dictatorship of the proletariat;
4) tricked the masses into invading the Great Hall of the People, attacking security officers, burning police cars and fire engines, and setting buildings ablaze;
5) was a small minority with ulterior motives, using the pretext of honouring Zhou Enlai to attack the party Central Committee headed by Mao Zedong; and
6) caused turmoil which, had it not been resolutely repressed by the iron fist of the proletarian dictatorship, would have allowed a small gang of anti-party, anti-socialist, bad elements to restore capitalism in China; and the whole country would have had to suffer that again.
7) Therefore, the people had to stand fast in solidarity with the party centre headed by Mao Zedong and struggle resolutely against counter-revolutionary turmoil.

Our present *April Student Movement* is said to be,

1) a planned conspiracy, an anti-party, anti-socialist turmoil;
2) slanderously attacking the leaders of party and State;
3) essentially contradicting the leadership of the CCP and the socialist system;
4) tricking the masses into attacking and injuring policemen;
5) a small minority with ulterior motives, using the opportunity to honour Hu Yaobang as a pretext for undermining the confidence of the people and stirring up trouble in the country; and

6) causing turmoil which, if allowed to run its course, will cause serious confusion and destroy China's radiant future; so it must be repressed in the cause of peace.
7) Therefore, people must quickly distinguish right from wrong and act resolutely to stop the turmoil.

Three years after the April Fifth Movement, comrade Deng Xiaoping said, "Many of the people died in the Tiananmen incident. We cannot very well say that it was counter-revolutionary." Today, and in a similar vein, we seriously say to the nation and to the world,

"So many youth and students have joined the April Student Movement, and it has the support of so many of the people, how can it be an anti-party, anti-socialist turmoil?"

Each Movement can be seen as both Patriotic and Democratic, representing the awakening and growth of the self-consciousness of the Chinese people. They are both great historical events that propel China forwards in the process of modernization. Yet the present Movement is greater, deeper, more rational and more constructive than the April Fifth Movement. This is demonstrated by the fact that Beijing's students and citizens have not angrily set fire to vehicles, nor have they beaten up any of the running dogs suppressing the masses. They have risen above that mediocre mentality of simply wanting a good bureaucrat to replace the bad one — which was the demand of the April Fifth Movement. This time the banner clearly upholds the supremacy of the Constitution, and criticises all activities that contravene it and the law. They rightly go beyond the limitations illegally imposed by local authorities, exercise their rights to freedom of speech and association, and demand reforms in the economic and political system. They demand structural reforms and the right for an effective supervision of government officials, with whom they want an equal and frank dialogue.

If this precious awakening of the self-consciousness of the youth, the intellectuals, and the people of China is suppressed as a riot, there will be no peace in the country. China will be excluded from the world community yet again, left alone to face the most dangerous of crises.

May 1, 1989

VI: On One-Party Dictatorship [12]

It is truly said that China is practicing capitalism under the name of socialism. A handful of people have usurped the central authority and now exercise a one party dictatorship. What is commonly called "state ownership" is actually the ownership of this small group, who profit themselves by abusing their power in business transactions, exploiting the people in the name of the State. To sustain their rule they trample on law, distort public opinion, appoint their children and grand-children to important positions, and deceive the public through direct control of the media. They share power with those who will support them, mouthpieces who "voluntarily wear chains, and put chains upon others." They force people to subscribe to the Four Cardinal Principles, including the insistence upon the "leadership of the Party," which by itself has generated a deep alienation and indifference amongst the population.

If the people will "do whatever the party asks," then they merely demonstrate the degree to which they have been fooled. The party's so-called "unified consciousness" and "unified leadership" of the "whole people" is nothing but lies. An independent person does not blindly submit his/her opinion to that of another. Therefore, I will support the CCP only when it is correct, according to the revised principle of "supporting the party leadership *when it is correct.*"

According to the party, the future will be complex. In literature, the blossoming of "a hundred flowers" will be the norm. In the economy, different systems will co-exist.[13] Yet, in spite of this, the political system is to remain under monopolistic control, nicely justified by the CCP as "unity with diversity." No matter what you call it, it is totally unconvincing, giving us only a supposedly-free person dancing on the end of a chain. The only route to democracy is the end of the one party dictatorship, and the establishment of genuinely democratic institutions — such as unofficial "unions." For democracy and freedom, the power to make laws must belong to the people; and that is the only way to guarantee freedom of speech and freedom of the press.

The shortcomings of a one-party dictatorship are:

1) It cannot police itself, which means that internal corruption grows into widespread crisis.
2) Inefficiency.
3) It has a poor analytical viewpoint and cannot appreciate the complexity of things. Therefore, its reforms are always piecemeal and inadequate. Lacking competing parties, it lauds itself for its petty achievements, and cannot recognise its mistakes.

Nixon was forced to resign over the Watergate incident in the USA. In Japan, Takeshita met the same fate in a bribery scandal. In China, however, collective responsibility is the principle of government; which leads one to ask: Why did not Li Peng resign along with Hu Yaobang [in 1987] as a demonstration of sincerity?

I think that the only way to change the present system is to struggle diligently for democracy, to which end we must insist that all are equal before the law, and that nobody is above the law. This means that laws should not be the product of the will of a few, but should be the genuine manifestation of the will of the people, in whose hands must lie the legislative power.

The main aim of law is to achieve freedom and equality. Freedom can be realised only when all submit to a law which reflects the common will of the people. Democratic politics will replace the evils of this neo-feudalistic society only when we replace its legal system. Government should execute the will of the people, from whom its power is drawn. If the National People's Congress is to perform this task, then the one-party electoral system must be changed.

Without genuine supervision by the people, government is inevitably corrupt. So let us fight for a new beginning of genuine democracy and freedom.

May 2, 1989

VII: X.X. Yeung,[14] For a Socialist Multi-Party System in China

Received opinion presents the multi-party system as a monopoly of capitalism, and has nothing to do with socialism. There are democratic socialist countries like Sweden, but then we are told that they are not really practicing socialism — with arguments that are not persuasive. Hungary now has a multi-party system as part of its political agenda, and Poland is talking about diversification. The East Germans accuse them of being revisionist. And in other communist-ruled countries, including the USSR and the PRC, the rationale of a multi-party system is rejected.

Chinese leaders argue that the multi-party system contradicts the Chinese reality. I recognise that the position of the CCP is all-powerful, but that is not very convincing as a reason for rejecting the existence of other political parties in China — truly independent organizations and democratic parties. My preliminary thoughts on the question are as follows:

1) If capitalism can have a multi-party system, why not socialism? I can see many reasons for having one. Party politics is, in the first place, the common political form of modern civilised society. So long as there are different interests in society, different political parties will naturally come into existence. A multi-party system is based on this.

The CCP has long insisted that under socialism people have common interests, and use this to justify a one-party dictatorship. However, the fact is that the interests of people in a socialist country are not always the same. There are different interest groups. In China there are at least four distinct interests: workers, peasants, merchants, and intellectuals. This is a "class" basis for different political parties. The CCP claim to represent everybody is not true. It simply cannot do it. Moreover, it has developed into a party alienated from the people, practicing bureaucratic rule. In modern China there is not a single representative institution.

The CCP is the only political party in China (excluding Taiwan), with the so-called democratic parties being branches of the CCP. Without competition, the communists' rule will never be at risk, will be able to do anything they want, and become totally corrupted. Putting its own interests before those of the people, the CCP enjoys unlimited privileges which it is frightened of losing. Hence its opposition to a multi-party system, and reference to the "Chinese reality," is an unconvincing argument.

However, history is always progressing, and attempts to reverse history are futile. A multi-party system with various checks and balances will develop in response to the variety of interests in China.

2) Some people worry that a multi-party system will alter the nature of the socialist state. This kind of worry is unfounded. Hasn't the nature of the capitalist state remained unchanged in spite of the multi-party system? This is because diverse interests can share a common ideology. That is, different parties may represent different interests, but share a fundamental belief in capitalism. Could the same logic not be applicable to socialism?

In theory a socialist society is the most humane, democratic, prosperous and rational society, forsaking all corrupt and decadent elements of the past. At this stage socialism is far from perfect, but as a developing system, improving itself, the people will naturally be attracted towards it. A multi-party system would protect socialism against those who would destroy it. So a socialist multi-party system has a pragmatic value, and we should regard its implementation as an obvious necessity.

3) More than seventy years after the establishment of the first socialist country by the Great October Revolution of 1917, we are faced with the unpleasant fact that all of the socialist countries lag behind the capitalist countries. Socialist countries are, generally speaking, poor and undemocratic. It is not surprising, therefore, that some people say that socialism is feudalism, and is regressive.

The ruling parties of most socialist countries are now beginning to wake up to the situation. Reform sweeps through the USSR, Europe, China and Vietnam. The reforms themselves are a declaration of past failures. Some achievements were certainly made, but new problems have arisen, creating difficulties everywhere. Faith in socialism has been shattered, and people everywhere turn blindly towards western capitalism.

Why are so many problems arising even when these countries undertake reform? Probably because the reforms are not sufficiently comprehensive. Almost without exception they focus on reform of the economic realm whilst their political structure remains the same. Inevitably a stagnant politics hampers the development of the economic sector. Only political reform can ease the difficulties and crisis facing the socialist countries.

The most critical feature of political reform must be the implementation of democracy. Without democracy, corruption will remain, and economic development will be inhibited. Under a one-party dictatorship, democracy must be bestowed on the people by those in power, who also have the power to withdraw it. There-fore, genuine democracy can only be realised through political diversification, the superior form of which is a socialist multi-party system.

4) The superiority of a socialist multi-party system is obvious, although there is doubt concerning its applicability to China. That reservation is certainly justified under the present determination of the CCP not to share power. However, the people will not be content with the *status quo;* but neither can the party itself. Corruption is causing serious trouble, and growing popular discontent threatens the party's legitimacy. The current Student Movement causes great alarm because it threatens to create a multi-party system.

It is certain that the CCP will not allow a new party even if it proclaims itself socialist, for it would be competitive. Accused of being counter-revolutionary, it would be made illegal and disbanded. Does that mean that we are helpless? Certainly not. We could win over the existing "democratic parties," and it would be embarrassing for the CCP to deny them their independence. The worst they could do would be to refuse financial support, which would be replaced by the people and overseas compatriots if they were genuinely independent.

Comrades in the democratic parties are believers in socialism. Their independence is a precondition for a multi-party system in China, and that is where her future modernization and democratization lies.

May 12, 1989

VIII: Some Thoughts on the Chinese Communist Party [15]

At present China is in serious trouble and faces many difficulties. This has made it necessary for us to analyze carefully the monopoly rule of the CCP over recent decades. The conclusion of this examination is that most of the mistakes made in China can be traced back to the basic principles of the Party. The details are as follows:

Ideologically, the CCP upholds the Four Cardinal Principles as some predetermined truth upon which all theoretical considerations are based. As an organization with a common conviction, some commonly embraced principles are to be expected in the Party. But it is absurd to force the people of the whole country to accept and defend these principles. Take for example the statement, "insist on the leadership of the Communist Party." Every political party hopes, by implementing its political programme, to win the support of the people. But it has to be realised through the common will of the people (through a general election). It is ridiculous to force upon the people some subjective and self-fulfilling wish as an eternal truth, and to demand that the whole country either toe the line, or face the "big stick" and the "tall hat" (i.e., repression). The dozens of mistakes made in the ideological conflict, and the loss of an independent personality among the intellectuals, are proof of this absurdity. The creativity of the Chinese is seriously hampered by this heavy burden. They are held back because they must follow the views of a small number of people.

In terms of organizational principle and form, the Communist Party has become an excellent breeding ground of dictatorial rule and bureaucratic politics, the latter being a standard result and natural extension of the former. The secretive and military methods of the war years linger on. "The individual submits to the organization, the junior submits to the senior, the party submits to the party central, and the party central submits to one person (or a few)." In short, "to obey orders is the highest duty." How can such a rigid organization not become a breeding ground of dictatorship, patriarchy, and the personality cult. Absence of democracy, and dictatorship by an individual, is realised through mass terror, as in the Cultural Revolution and the downfall of Hu Yaobang. This dictatorship always begins inside the party, and in a one-party State like ours it is only natural that it become a permanent phenomenon. There are today people who rest their hopes on one or two benevolent personages in the party. Such a thought is terrifying. Have we not had enough of the time when we place the lives of one billion people into the hands of one or two individuals.

"Our great party will always redress all wrongs in the end." On the basis of this oft-quoted statement, one billion people have lost decades of their lives, tens of millions have been killed, and civilization was thrown backward hundreds of years — as occurred during the Cultural Revolution, and in Stalin's purges. If a party has spent the greater part of its existence committing inexcusable errors, what kind of gamble is it to place in its hands the destiny of one billion people?

The CCP also has the practice of picking out for punishment "a handful" of bad elements; so why doesn't it select a large handful from the party? If 80% of the party members are good (measured against the average moral standard of a common citizen), what shall we do about the 20%, which is about ten millions? Are they not a large "handful" who should be punished?

The Communist Party's position within the country's political structure is also ambiguous. Theoretically, all power has belonged to the people and their representatives in the National People's Congress since October 1, 1949, with everyday administration exercised by the Government. In practice, however, the whole country has always been under a one-party leadership. The political programme of the CCP is not supported by a nation-wide general election, nor is the party's will produced by the National People's Congress. Rather, it controls what the Constitution calls the "highest institutional power" (i.e., the National People's Congress) and the "highest executive organ" (i.e., the State Council). If both the Congress and the Council are merely vehicles of power for the CCP, what does the word "highest" mean here? If the elected People's Congress is merely for the convenience of the party, why bother to say, "All power to the people"? It is more appropriate to speak of power to the party, or the party's army. A party member who does not hold any governmental office [i.e., Deng Xiaoping] can decide, in a few statements, the country's policy in the coming years, which means that this one man's view is equal to those of one billion people. Isn't this shocking and sickening?

We keep hearing that party norms have been transgressed. Is this not because party members are given all kinds of priority and privileges? If they were just like ordinary citizens there would be no problem. Those who have joined the party in recent years, however, are living proof of the replacement of political commitment by pursuit of privilege. Why should they have more than ordinary citizens? And why should the public treasury support the party, rather than its members' contributions? Without that, would we still have a budget deficit? The dark side of our economy is "officials abusing power in return for bribes," whilst the old men who are our political leaders suck the blood of the nation.

Our country needs leadership, but it should be chosen by the people. A party ought to win the support of the people before it forms the government and implements a programme. In short, everything should be decided by the people.

If a citizen does not have the right to express her/his opinion, then s/he does not have an obligation to obey the government. Following this logic, when a political party appoints itself as the representative of the people, is not elected by the people, and has lost all its confidence, the people do not have a duty to support or even to pay any attention to it.

The order of our priorities should be: the People, the State and Government, and finally the Party. It should not be the other way round, where the Party is everything, and represents nothing.

May 17, 1989

IX: Hue Yu, [16] Hoping for a Brighter Future

Since the establishment of the Republic by the CCP in 1949 we have always thought that the main contradiction in society was that between the backwardness of our productive forces and the growing material and cultural needs of the people. However, this belief is based upon the deception of propaganda. The main contradiction at this time is the conflict between democracy and autocracy, between the rule of law and the rule of man; and therein lies the reason mainland China has not been able to catch up to the rest of the world.

Never resolved in any meaningful way, that contradiction must generate turmoil in our society whenever it deepens. It is the reason for all of the disruptions in the past, in spite of attempts to lay the blame at the door of "counter-revolutionary cliques." Turmoil, in fact, is a means of preventing the contradiction getting worse; and that too can be said of the Democracy Movement. When we hear the same old song and dance about class struggle and that the Pa-triotic-Democratic Movement is disruptive, it all sounds very familiar. However, if this leads merely to a defusing of the situation, then the spirit of the Movement will have been betrayed.

How are we best to understand the Democracy Movement?

First, note that the students who constitute the main force of the Democracy Movement have generated some false notions. Remember the comment in the *People's Daily*, that some students promoted the slogan, "Down with the Communist Party!" The newspaper seized upon that as the basis of its April 26th editorial. In order to clarify the situation, on April 27th students held up banners unanimously stating, "Support the Communist Party!" Such a response implied, however, that the students support the one-party hierarchy of the CCP. In reality, one of the elements in democracy is to allow dissent. In terms of politics, it means the existence of many parties who might form the government. You cannot, as the students were doing, ask for freedom and democracy through a compromise with autocracy; and such false thinking leads nowhere. Therefore, in the discussions between government officials and student representatives, the persistent deadlock should be explained by that, not by the insincerity of government officials.

The harboring of erroneous ideas that run counter to the spirit of democracy, freedom, science and the rule of law, as manifested by the students themselves, should be seriously considered. It is a weakness that can be fatal. Student organization is loose, and their representatives are not always dependable. The appearance of certain bureaucratic phenomena has been disappointing, and has led to the disillusionment of some overseas Chinese. That such problems exist is amply demonstrated by the withdrawal of Wang Dan and Wuer Kaixi from the leadership of ASUBU.

Even worse is the fact that some students have adopted feudalistic policies to fight for democracy. Before the Chairman of the National People's Congress, Wan Li, returned from his trip outside China, there were many people placing their hopes in him as the "incorruptible magistrate." Once again, we are looking for a master, a single individual to whom we can link our fate. Mao Zedong once said that Deng Xiaoping was useful, but that he should not be given power. "He is a wolf in the high mountains and, once he is given power, he runs wild." However, since there are no legal checks, nobody is able to escape from the ability to run wild when in power. Our experiences under Mao and Deng should serve as a constant reminder of that. A leader who acts properly may be permitted to continue as a leader, but life-long leadership can never be allowed. In the latter event, the poison of feudalism floods over modern society.

We can all see that in China the people who are under the iron fist of arbitrary rule and slavery are not the students, but the workers, peasants and other strata of society. In the Democracy Movement the students, who have had greater freedom than others, are making the loudest demands for democracy and freedom. This should change, and the people who should speak are not students, but the people.

We know that the tradition of China is, "The victors become kings, and the vanquished become bandits." That is because, throughout Chinese history, there was no rule of law. In modern society there is no necessity for politics to be a life or death struggle. The progress of history is in fact the transformation from individualism to contract. Contract is law; and its key feature is the enabling of a political struggle in which opponents check each other. The checks come from the exercise of democratic political rights; and the guarantee of personal security is the precondition of those rights.

Students are not independent personalities, being economically dependent on others; and their role in society is temporary. Therefore, their voice is never very strong. At best they can form a vanguard, a herald, speaking on behalf of social development. The fact that the government treats them with such indifference demonstrates the point.

Some have argued that the students can rely on overseas financial backing to carry on the struggle. However, democracy is both a means and an end. It is doubtful whether a countervailing force could be developed whilst depending on other people's help for economic security. Foreign help is a factor, but the decisive ones must be internal. Sun Yatsen sought overseas help in his struggle for democracy, and failed. Mao, on the other hand, was victorious.

[undated]

X: Ma Siufang,[17] Statement of a Tiananmen Hunger Striker

The students' Patriotic-Democratic Movement asserted in April that its main tasks were, i) the initiation of political reforms in China; ii) protecting the civil rights and liberty defined in the Constitution; and iii) ensuring the smooth implementation of economic reforms. With these in mind, tens of thousands of students have been staying in Beijing for a month-long public demonstration, hunger-strike and sit-in, in order to persuade the government, through these peaceful activities, to undertake a critical review of the ten-year old [economic] reform programme. They urge the government to investigate the mistakes and drawbacks of the reforms and to take legal action against corrupt leaders in the government. At the same time, the students demand that the government take immediate action against serious corruption among bureaucrats and others. However, the "feudalistic absolutism" of the government, faced with the students' reasonable demands and peaceful expression of discontent, chooses to take a fraudulent and high-handed attitude — ignoring the dignity of the country. In government statements, such as the April 26th editorial and the speeches of May 20th, and by constantly delaying a "dialogue," again and again, the government suffocates and scorns the Patriotic-Democratic Movement. It makes use of news censorship and an incredibly large amount of news distortion to blur the real picture of the Movement. All those righteous, responsible compatriots concerned with Chinese democratization become doubtful, and ask, What are the students trying to do?

However, their dishonesty will not last long. Ultimately, the corrupt government will not be able to hide its ugly face and distorted mouth from the people. At this time the people in Beijing are bravely surging to the streets, and shouting, "Down With Li Peng." Clearly, the previously silent and serene Chinese are awakening. This signifies the imminent advance of Chinese democracy.

The recent series of events plainly show the deep despair of the Chinese people over the feudalistic absolutism. The tragic fact of the hunger strike totally destroys any remnant of faith in the good intentions of the government. At last, the people rise up. April's Student-Patriotic-Democratic Movement has now become May's Popular-Patriotic-Democratic Movement. No matter what the outcome, this Movement is certainly a new page in Chinese history, a milestone in Chinese progress.

At the present stage of the Movement, what are the tasks ahead? Are they just the ending of martial law and downfall of Li Peng? We want these things, to clear away obstacles to democratization, which is our ultimate goal. Moreover, the call for the downfall of Li Peng is a concrete move against corruption in the bureaucracy, not just a pure slogan.

The first important task of the people is to exterminate corruption in the government. The cause of this deterioration in the government is "feudalistic absolutism." Therefore, breaking absolutism is an essential goal of the Movement. Only if all-round political reform can be effectively and urgently implemented can corruption be removed and our nation made strong. To hand this task over to corrupted bureaucrats would be a historical farce, and this splendid Popular Democratic Movement would fail and fade out.

To overthrow absolutism and to strive for democracy we must do following:

First, we should activate our civil capacity in the State through the promotion of a strong sense of our civil and political rights. The present absolutism deprives the people of their electoral rights, to vote and to be elected. The citizens cannot freely choose the candidates and, thereby, the right to be elected is lost. This leads to the situation of where the National People's Congress (NPC) is a rubber stamp, and the government is corrupt. Our citizens should no longer accept the corruption and oppression of our government. We must rise up and strive for our civil rights as they are defined in the Constitution.

Second, citizens should have the right to check the operations of the government; i.e., the right of political participation. After ten years of [economic] reform, we now should not be silent. We need real political reforms, not slogans. As long as the CCP does not introduce a fundamental political reform, we should not cease our struggle. As long as our constitutionally-guaranteed civil rights are not guaranteed, we cannot rest. Our nation should no longer be silenced by political machinations.

Third, we should strive for a democratic administration and the end of patriarchal feudal methods. If we are proud of our ancient culture, then we should now recognise that the existing, brutal patriarchal system is most destructive of it. The Chinese myth of the good ruler has been broken since the death of Mao Zedong. Whoever desires to establish it again opposes the will of the people. We have no reason to retain this patriarchal system, and 1.1 billion people no longer must put the fate of our country in the hands of a senile 85-year-old. Gerontocratic politics must be ended by this Popular Democratic Movement; and the life-long tenure of office for cadres must end. Otherwise, democracy will never take root in our country, and we will fester in feudalistic absolutism, with only the corrupt bureaucrats standing to benefit.

Fourth, we should abolish the rule of man and establish a rule of law. For thousands of years human rights and freedom of speech have not existed in China. The most distinctive characteristic of the [Confucian] "rule of good men" was a poor legal system. Powerful bureaucrats could not be punished. This is still the situation in China. Huge errors and losses have been produced during the last ten years of reform. The Li Peng group should be held legally responsible. But Li's group boldly requires the people to suffer whilst they deny all responsibility. This is the miserable outcome of the rule of man, which must be totally rejected if our country is to avoid the unacceptable consequences.

Fifth, we should abolish press censorship. Freedom of the press is the first step towards democracy. If this is not there, we can only have a pseudo-democracy. The voices of the people, the sincere criticism of the corrupt government, cannot be heard. Today, we should have a check on the government, to fight against the monster; and that check is a free press. The press should express truth and the will of the people.

Sixth, we must get rid of elitist politics and set up people's justice. The first priority of the current ruling group is the preservation of its authority without reference to the will of the people. Only a popular politics can place the people's welfare to the fore. And the homespun argument that, "someone must be rich first," is a mere excuse for the privileged classes in authority.

In a nutshell, the hope of our national State lies on the path of democratization. Without it, we have nothing. All those government and party personnel who oppose this principle will be opposed by the people, and must eventually be buried under the surging tides of the Popular Democratic Movement.

Our people unite together in this Patriotic-Democratic Movement. We must build the basis for the nation-State; and the task of nation-building is ours. Let us join together to take up the burden.

May 24, 1989

XI: Tian Chun,[18] A Critique of ASUBU

Many people have come to realise that the main problem with the current Movement is a lack of cohesive organization, as shown in a confusing movement of staff, ineffective command, disorderly assignment of tasks, and a low level of efficiency. A further drawback is the rather undemocratic nature of the organization, with power concentrated in the hands of a few people who are isolated from the public. In the early days of the Movement many valuable opinions were prevented from being communicated to the decision-makers. This has led to faulty decision-making and considerably weakened the general public's confidence in the Movement and in the students.

Organizational defects show themselves in the absence of necessary departments (such as an Overseas Liaison Department), and the lack of cooperation between decision-making and the execution of policies. The student leaders get buried in details and cannot concentrate on strategic decisions that should be made by them. For example, the question whether or not the students should withdraw from the Square affected the entire Movement. Therefore, after the decision had been made not to retreat, discipline in the Square should have been maintained by various means. The implementation of the decision should have been arranged.

Moreover, the organizers tend to forget the public because of an over-concentration on events in the Square. For example, a few days after the [May 13th] beginning of the hunger strike, support for the students from the populace reached a peak. However, we kept our attention directed at the Square and the hunger strikers, ignoring the need to make propaganda in the factories and on the streets, organising the masses — with some of us innocently disapproving of the workers going on strike. With so many people out on the streets, we failed to inspire and guide them. We were so involved in the mobilization of the masses, that we made that an end in itself. This was an emotional indulgence. In addition to that emotion, there was fear, expressed in the underestimation of the power and consciousness of the crowd, and our ability to control the situation. So when the crowd appeared, ironically, we became afraid and confused, and failed to look to the next stage of our Movement; that is, we were not daring enough and hesitated to join hands with the crowd.

Another important strategic mistake that we made was to call upon the students and citizens to block the army trucks. Even if the citizens went out to block the trucks on their own initiative, we should have dispersed them. Since the government had made the mistake itself in ordering the army into Beijing, we should have let it go farther down this wrong path. The farther it went, the more advantageous to us. (The fact is, the army would not dare to stage a bloody crackdown against the students and citizens. The main purpose of their coming into Beijing is rather to prevent the activity of the Zhao Ziyang's supporters in the party). Concentrating upon establishing a blockade against the trucks, we have neglected the education and mobilization of the masses. Therefore, once the troops retreated, we became inactive in anti-climactic response.

Therefore, we can recognise a lack of general policy and organizational purpose in the Movement, which is to be seen as both blind and passive. On the other hand, the problem can be solved by establishing a democratic and efficient leading organization, uniting the various elements in the Movement. This is the problem that we are now working to solve.

The Movement is reduced. The enthusiasm of the people and the students has lessened, deceived by the government's manipulation, and the public's failure to give a strong response to the students' demonstration. This regression is caused by ourselves, however, and may also be ended by putting in more of our effort.

An analysis of this situation can be made from three analytical perspectives: the government, the general public and the students.

1) The government is now regarded as one which is controlled by our opponents. Yang Shangkun's and Li Peng's May 20th

speeches were full of hostility, but these statements isolated them. The reason why they can gain the upper hand is that they are in control of the military and the propaganda machinery. They have two main opponents. The first are the so-called Reformists led by Zhao Ziyang, with supporters in the party, government and the military. They are not to be dismissed lightly. The second, as we know so well, is the group composed of the students and the general public.

Using the propaganda machinery the government tries to downplay the power struggle within the party, but it remains. The government is very weak, very scared. This can be illustrated by the meager support reported by the mass media every day. On the other hand, they are preparing themselves, getting themselves ready for "war." As Yang Shangkun said, they cannot retreat. Retreat means, "Down with the Communist Party." Here, the party refers to a handful of people. So — either the fish die or the net breaks. If we do not get free, what little we have achieved out of this Movement, along with the future of China, will be crushed.

2) As for the people in Beijing, their enthusiasm has decreased. There are people who need our support and inspiration, waiting for our renewed efforts. When the time comes, they will stand on our side. A small group of citizens and workers has already joined us. We must actively strengthen this kind of bond. Whenever danger appears, we have to help them. This is the best policy for promoting our goals. The tactic of the government is to separate people and workers from the students, and to deal with them separately; and that must not be permitted to succeed.

In addition, there are the intellectuals and the support from overseas. The intellectuals are still carrying out their struggle with a hunger strike to be launched tomorrow. Those who are prominent will not easily give up their fight, and those who have been less prominent almost all support the students, and are simply awaiting new opportunities. On the other hand, overseas support has always been very concerned over the students' ability to organise themselves effectively and stand firm. Demonstrable organizational ability will strengthen overseas support and produce a continuation of material aid.

Moreover, the Movement is nation-wide, with Beijing as the pioneer. The whole nation is watching Beijing. Therefore, we must quickly end this anti-climactic depression and let the burning fires of Beijing spread through the whole country.

3) Students are perhaps the most important aspect of the Movement, and a display of low morale is always disappointing. Due to insufficient organization and promotion, many students are scattered. This condition must not continue. On the one hand, promotion must be carried out more vigorously and, on the other, the students' own organization must also be strengthened. At the moment, the link between the student organizers and the ordinary students seems to be broken. Beijing University had a division-of-responsibility committee, which must have been dissolved. It relied mainly on broadcasting, but that medium is limited, and liaison units must be immediately established, or a mass meeting of students held in the near future. Generally speaking, the students' present situation is as follows: Although there may be some pessimistic elements among our organizers, we must present a united front and a determination to see things through to the end. We must make this decision for ourselves, recognising that success or failure depends upon the moves that we make.

This attempt to analyze different aspects of the situation, in general, notes that the situation at this time is relatively quiet. This is a very crucial moment, for we still have the opportunity to reorganize ourselves and renew our strength. Also, we should realise that if we persist, unyielding, faced also with the pressure of world-wide commentary, even this foolish government will be forced to compromise. The contraction of foreign investment and the public's withdrawal of bank deposits, are aspects of an economic ultimatum that will directly influence government interests and make them reconsider. We must not relax!

Basically, our goal is to promote the process of democratization in China, and to lead her onto the road of prosperity. Specific demands which will realise this main purpose are seen in the call for a free press and the punishment of corrupt officials. As the movement develops, specific demands will change continuously as well. For example, we began with a request for an audience with the government; and then demands for the resignation of Li Peng, the recall of the National People's Congress

(NPC) and the termination of martial law took predominance. Through it all, however, we must not lose sight of the chief task, whatever might have been achieved. And what have we achieved? Apart from awakening the masses, not much; which is one good reason for keeping going!

Having clearly defined our general goal, it becomes more possible and appropriate to talk about the immediate tasks of our Movement. What we most urgently need to do is form a better organization, with ASUBU taking the lead and presenting itself as a model. At the same time, the following concrete measures should be given due attention by the Movement's organizers:

1) Launch an information programme to combat government propaganda.
2) Try to help the workers who have been arrested.
3) Improve discipline in the Square.
4) Begin preparations for the NPC, including meetings with members of the NPC, and drafting a general report on the Movement. We must not place much hope in the NPC, but it will be an opportunity to renew the strength of our struggle.

It is most important also to realise that we have two kinds of tactical actions to follow. One is active, with planning, preparation and execution. The other is passive, which involves taking advantage of events over which we have no control; for example, announcing support of a hunger strike by intellectuals, or using the government's attempt to manipulate the workers into an anti-student movement as an opportunity for renewed struggle.

Now there is a question to be answered: Is ASUBU the leader of the Universities in Beijing or of the whole nation? For now, its duties centre on Beijing. However, in terms of direction and spirit, it bears the responsibility of directing the Movement of the whole nation, and is waiting for the right time to set up an Autonomous Students' Union of China to take over its duties. What we can be sure of at this moment is that the ASUBU should have the whole nation in mind and should not adopt any policies based on localism and parochialism.

For the Movement to have reached its present state, we have already paid a painful price, and yet the fruits are few. To make our past tears and sweat worthwhile and to save China from the black hand of a few schemers, to live up to our conscience and to history, we should persevere, persevere until a new dawn arrives.

June 1, 1989

XII: *Su Shaozhi,*[20] *The Origin and Results of China's 1989 Democracy Movement*

"Truth will inevitably defeat sheer power. Righteousness will eventually eradicate evil." This is the opening sentence of an essay that I wrote in 1988 in memory of Bukharin's execution fifty years earlier.

Today the USSR has rehabilitated the victims of the Great Terror of the thirties; Hungary has done the same with Imre Nagy, the victim of events there in 1956; and in Poland Solidarity has been made legal, with its members being elected to the national assembly. While these socialist countries advanced gradually along the road of democracy, humanism and rationalism, the sound of gunfire and the rumble of tanks were the harsh sounds echoing through Beijing on the night of June 3-4, 1989. The so-called People's Liberation Army suppressed the students' and citizens' peaceful Democracy Movement with armed force, with a massacre followed by mass arrests and executions, producing shocked criticism around the world.

Characteristics

The 1989 Democracy Movement was a dynamic and peaceful mass movement unprecedented in Chinese history; and its repression by the *people's* government and the *people's* army was just as unique.

Today the world is so integrated by systems of mass communication that it is impossible to isolate people from the news. Consequently, falsehoods and lies are increasingly fabricated to create doubts concerning the deaths in Tiananmen Square. The number of deaths is, of course, important; but even more important is the fact that the government and PLA fired on their own people. Deng Xiaoping said on June 9th that, "If tanks have rolled through the

Square, then the difference between right and wrong is confused in this country." The fact remains, however, that guns and tanks were to be found in the square, and their presence declared the government's loss of legitimacy.

Debate is no longer necessary, and we must now make an objective analysis of the Democracy Movement and its military repression. Its main characteristics were:

1) *Endurance.* During the fifty day period between Hu's death on April 15th to the armed repression of June 3rd-4th, in spite of ups and downs, the scope of the Movement never decreased.

2) *Massive size.* Initiated by the Beijing students as a Student Movement, people joined from all strata of society, developing it into a massive, peaceful Democracy Movement. From Beijing it spread to universities in other cities (e.g., Guangzhou, Shanghai, Xian); from the universities to the larger intellectual community (educational, technological-scientific, literary and journalistic circles); and from there to the whole society, involving mass organizations like the Student Federation, the National Women's Federation, the democratic factions, even the Central Party School and segments of the party hierarchy. The street demonstrations that were first organised by the student organizations, were supported by the citizens, and later joined by the citizens. Marches involved hundreds of thousands, even millions, of people. When the PLA first began to move into the city, they were blocked by those same citizens, including old people, women and children. Their spontaneous actions could not have been instigated by a "handful" of conspirators.

3) *Spontaneity.* Initially a spontaneous outburst, organizations gradually began to emerge, but too late to be effective. The government repeatedly asserted that it was an organised conspiracy; but the facts indicate that it was spontaneous and gradual development of an organization similar to Poland's Solidarity — embryonic in the examples of the Autonomous Students' Union of Beijing Universities, the Autonomous Students' Union of Foreign Universities, the Beijing Workers' Autonomous Federation, and the Autonomous Union of Beijing Intellectuals. Their formation alerted the authorities, who immediately declared them to be illegal. They were largely ineffective because they were organised too late, developed little strategy and tactics, and were often torn apart by internal disagreements.

4) *Non-violent.* Both students and citizens embraced peaceful means, with the students advising the citizens against destructive activities. For example, on May 23rd, when three people defaced Mao Zedong's portrait in Tiananmen Square, they were immediately taken to the police by the students. In early June, when there were clashes between citizens and soldiers, students protected the soldiers. There was an improved civility between citizens and students, as the overseas edition of the *People's Daily* indicated on May 23rd, in an article entitled "The current civic mentality of the Beijing people." Instead of taking advantage of this situation the government labelled the Movement "an organised conspiracy, a riot," in the April 26th editorial, initiating political pressures that eventually led to armed suppression. Bloodshed being the last resort of politicians, when the government resorted to violence it was demonstrating its frailty.

5) *Inner-party conflict.* In dealing with the Democracy Movement the highest levels of the party and government have been involved in a power struggle, and this immensely complicates the analysis. Ultimate decision-making power undoubtedly lies with Deng, who favoured economic reform, but is conservative in politics and ideology. Therefore, he must confront and make compromises with both reformers and hard-liners. Hard-liners used the Movement to put pressure on Deng, and reformers tried to use it to protect themselves. Faced with this conflict, the government was unable to work out a strategy, which is one of the reasons that the 1989 Movement was able to last so long in spite of its ups and downs. Since Deng labelled the Movement a "riot" from the very start, he had to compromise with the hard-liners, and move towards the use of force. Both the students and Deng became victims of forces beyond their control. Deng's image as a reformer, which had led former Chancellor Schmidt of West Germany to call him one of the greatest contemporary politicians, disappeared in an instant, as have his reforms.

6) *Military presence.* The government moved some 200,000 troops to Beijing, even whilst declaring that the troops were not meant for use against the students. It was not necessary to use soldiers and tanks against the unarmed and peaceful masses; and is linked rather to the power struggle in the party — establishing the unfortunate precedent of using the army to resolve such conflicts.

Because of these six features, in spite of opportunities for mitigating the situation, neither side behaved rationally, and compromise was impossible. However, the authorities were primarily responsible by declaring the Student Movement to be an organised conspiracy, a riot that had to be put down by military force, intimidating the masses by insisting upon the need to eradicate "liberalism",— and thereby making bloodshed and a national disaster inevitable.

The past is the teacher of the future. We must, therefore, remember these events and seek out a theoretical explanation.

Origins

Although initiated by the Student Movement, triggered by the event of Hu's death, the 1989 Democracy Movement has its origins further in the past.

Since it was established in 1949 the People's Republic of China has undeniably had many achievements; but numerous problems have also emerged. Movements and policies initiated by the party and government devastated the economy and produced popular dissatisfaction. These mistakes were not investigated or corrected until the extremes of the Cultural Revolution utterly destroyed the people's confidence and led them to press for democracy and reform. Since the Third Plenum of the Eleventh Central Committee of the CCP, ideological liberalization, an open door policy, and reforms have been widely advocated, and China has thereby had an opportunity to strengthen herself. However, because of the limitations of the old ideology and organization, they developed in a distorted manner. Nonetheless, changes were in the air and the demand for democracy could not be thwarted.

Deng Xiaoping understands this. In his June 9th speech he said, "International and domestic circumstances made this storm inevitable, independent of any human will." A proper analysis of the situation, and correct policies, could have produced a favorable conclusion. Unfortunately, an erroneous path was taken.

When considering the international situation we must take into account the whirlwind of events raised by the USSR and the East European countries, including the development of pluralism in a one-party system in the USSR and Hungary, the victory of Solidarity in the Polish elections, and the power demonstrated by the people in Asian countries like the Philippines, South Korea and Pakistan.

When considering the domestic situation in China herself, the important factors are as follows:

1) *The economic background.* Reforms moved away from the single unified system of nationalization and collectivization towards the creation of various modes of ownership. We now also have joint-stock enterprises (of Chinese and foreign firms), a private sector based on household enterprises, and cooperatives operating according to the [profit-based] "responsibility system." This has produced various interest groups in society in addition to the workers, peasants and intellectuals. Demands for political pluralism inevitably follow, as people want delegates in the National People's Congress who will represent their interests. Conceding to this demand is the first step towards democracy.

At the same time, the market economy produced demands for the elimination of monopolies and economic privileges, which were also expressed in a demand for democracy as the vehicle to this end. A new middle class is, therefore, the basis of the new Democracy Movement — the weakness of which is due to the fact that this class is not yet fully formed.[21] Nevertheless, economic reform will lead inevitably to political reform.

2) *Ideological developments.* Since 1987 the doctrinal monopoly of Marxism has been broken, and people are beginning to re-evaluate socialism and communism from the perspective of western ideas that are an inevitable product of the open door policy. The appearance of ideological pluralism has, however, led to a toughening of resistance to it. So, in 1981 we see the official criticism of the film, *Bitter Love;* in 1983 there was the "anti-spiritual pollution campaign;" and in 1987 the "anti-bourgeois liberalization" campaign. However, after each repression and brief period of silence, there was a reaction; and the 1989 Democracy Movement has emerged with tremendous force.

3) *Corruption.* Because of a failure to reform the political system, the ruling group has been able to use its privileges to make money, resulting in a concentration of power and wealth. Official profiteering, corruption and decadence increasingly characterise the CCP, government, and PLA organizations. As people's lives are made more difficult by inflation, so is this inequality felt more keenly by the people. Moreover, the development of unemployment, and the associated social contradictions, leads to a loss of confidence in the party and government and a desire to change the *status quo.* The immediate cause of the present political crisis was the students' strong

sense of corruption in the government, which was then supported by the masses, as it developed into a demand for democracy.

Economic, ideological and social forces all made the demand for democracy inevitable in the Chinese domestic situation.

Now the CCP is Marxist, and therefore supposedly concerned with the liberation of the individual. China is known as a *people's* republic, and its Constitution and government are said to be dedicated to the service of the people — granting freedom of speech and assembly. The students and the masses believed this, up to the point that they were so bloodily repressed. How could an act which so contradicts the principles of the legal system occur?

1) China's system is a mixture of Stalinism and feudal despotism. One of its characteristics is the unity of party-government-economy-military-culture-ideology into an indivisible hierarchy. This includes not only political machinery, but factories, schools, and all social organizations. Every government employee is absolutely subordinate to his/her superiors, not to the masses, at the peak of which pyramid is a single person around whom there must develop a personality cult. His power decides everything, without room for different opinions. Collegial leadership is a myth, not to mention democracy and legalism. Such a leadership cannot tolerate demonstrations and Movements of democracy and the citizens. Such a political system inevitably produces a powerful bureaucracy which, after forty years, cannot be easily overturned. The bureaucrats will oppose any measures that threaten them, justifying themselves with a Stalinist ideology.

2) Under this political system, economic reforms and the open door policy did bring economic improvements; but those with special privileges in the government distort those reforms, taking advantage of their power, and resisting political change — "economically anti-left, politically anti-right." It is worth noting that the privileged children of officials, who opposed the 1983 and 1987 campaigns, supported the hard-line policies of their parents in 1989.

3) Internal struggles at the highest levels of the CCP played a part in the political response to the Democracy Movement. The struggle between hardliners and moderates was resolved by the victory of the former, who regarded any compromise as a sign of weakness.

So, from the political perspective also the repression of the 1989 Democracy Movement was inevitable. That it was so bloody can be ascribed to tactical errors on both sides, the impotence of Li Peng's government, and the power struggle within the party.

Consequences

In history a similar situation to that which developed in China in the summer of 1989 is the Hungarian Revolution of 1956. Matyas Rakosi's government was bureaucratic and despotic, opposing the masses until the latter rose up against the small ruling group. Russian tanks suppressed that rebellion. The difference between the two situations is that in Hungary the main force was the working class, and the oppressors were foreign soldiers. At the time Mao Zedong stated that "part of the [Hungarian] masses had been deceived by counter-revolutionary forces inside and outside the country." Thirty years later we see the rehabilitation of the Hungarian uprising, the rehabilitation of the executed leader, Imre Nagy, who is now called a "martyr for democracy and a national hero." In this example we see that truth will be victorious.

Military force has temporarily crushed the 1989 Movement. Yet it stimulated the political awakening and democratic thoughts of every Chinese, making us aware that we can no longer remain in the worsening circumstances of totalitarian government. Spreading like wildfire, this underground ideology is sowing the seeds of an even greater future Movement. The bloodshed also destroyed the authority of the CCP, of the government, of Marxist socialism, all of which have lost their future credibility.

In the short term:

1) Suppression, arrests and executions lead to a loss of popular support; while all the propaganda justifying it leads to popular alienation. Apathy and non-cooperation surface, and confidence in the authorities can not be renewed.

2) The victory of the hardliners produces an economic re-centralization, taking the country backwards ten to twenty years, reintroducing methods that have already proven themselves to be bankrupt.

3) The 1989 Movement demonstrated the necessity of punishing corruption severely. This is a positive consequence. In July, 1989, the Politburo announced the need to further de-Stalinize and pro-

hibit the children of officials entering commercial ventures. Whether this can be implemented, however, is doubtful.

4) Suffering from inflation, a decline in foreign tourism and foreign loans consequent upon the repression, agricultural shortages and production slowdown, all indicate an intensification of the economic crisis in China.

5) Economic crisis will intensify the power struggle within the party, starting with a new round of struggles between Deng and the economic hardliners. Once Deng dies this struggle will be intensified.

6) Military suppression cannot but influence the policy of "one country, two systems," referring to the Sino-British agreement whereby the administration of Hong Kong will be turned over to the PRC in 1997. The agreement cannot be cancelled, but the middle and upper classes will drain the colony of capital, jeopardizing future prosperity. The possibility for a future agreement with Taiwan has been reduced to a minimum.

As for the long run implications, the very existence of Marxist theory and practice in the PRC is threatened. The official leadership has failed to solve the main problems facing the PRC, and obviously distorts reality with inappropriate concepts. Unable to break with a disreputable past, they are incapable of analyzing the problems with which they are now faced. They called the Movement a counter-revolutionary riot, which is obviously mistaken.

Meanwhile, the masses and the healthy elements in the CCP are helpless, for China lacks the fundamental prerequisite for productive analysis — which is free and independent exploration by means of various complicated theories, which in their scientific independence need not bow to the official ideology. By contrast, to have no frank opinion, to be dominated by the official media, to have ideological leaders interfering constantly, to be permitted only to praise those leaders, whilst severely punishing dissidents — such is the present situation.

The 1989 Democracy Movement and its suppression is a world-historical event. If China is to develop towards democracy, then she must modernize by reform and openness. It is, therefore, essential that the Movement be properly understood by the CCP, the Chinese masses, Marxists, socialists, and all progressive people who seek democracy and justice.

[undated]

NOTES

1. Born in 1965, Wang Dan was a first year History student at Beijing University. A high profile figure in Tiananmen Square during the April-June events of 1989, he was top of the post-massacre wanted list put out by the government, and was arrested in Beijing in July, 1989, having failed to escape the country.

2. Wang is referring to the denunciation of Stalin and Stalinism at the 20th Congress of the Communist Party of the Soviet Union (CPSU) in 1956.

3. The Polish "event" refers to the necessity of the Soviet leadership accepting Gomulka as Polish leader in 1956. The Hungarian "event" is the Nagy regime in Hungary prior to its repression by Soviet tanks in 1956.

4. There is an important distinction between "private property" and "personal property" for anyone living in a socialist State. The former is bourgeois property, which can be used to employ the labour of others for the generation of a surplus; it is the fields, the factories, the workshops. Personal property is, by contrast, that which is possessed as a result of one's own non-exploitative work, be it a bicycle, an automobile, or a house.

5. Born in 1945, Ren Wanding is a graduate of the Beijing Agricultural and Engineering College. Imprisoned for four years (1979-1983) for his participation in the Democracy Wall Movement, he was working for the Beijing Equipment and Fixture Company when this pamphlet was written. Following the massacre of June 3-4 he was arrested.

6. The reader should note that Article 51 of the 1982 Chinese Constitution states, "The exercise by citizens of the People's Republic of China of their freedoms and rights may not infringe upon the interests of the state..."

7. These principles were first formulated in a speech by Deng Xiaoping at a party conference on theoretical work on March 30, 1979. The speech defined the four limits of opposition in the statement, "Activities against socialism, against proletarian dictatorship, against the leadership of the Party, against Marxism-Leninism and the Thought of

Mao Zedong...are prohibited according to the law and will be prosecuted."

8. The full title of this statement is, "The Historical Functions and Objective Goals of the People's Democracy Movement — Edited Speeches delivered at Five Institutions of Higher Education in Beijing, April 27-May 4, 1989."

9. Totally under the control of the CCP there are eight "democratic parties" in China, which are expected to promote official policy in society and through public statements in the Chinese People's Political Consultative Conference, which is convened simultaneously with the NPC. The parties are i) the Revolutionary Committee of the Guomindang (i.e., Nationalist Party), ii) the Democratic League, iii) the Democratic Construction Society, iv) the Promotion of Democracy Society, v) the Democratic Party of Workers and Peasants, vi) The Zigong Party, vii) the September 3rd Society, and viii) the League for Democratic Self-Government of Taiwan.

10. The "October Incident" was the arrest of the Maoist "Gang of Four," and the beginning of Deng Xiaoping's domination of the body politic and introduction of economic reforms.

11. Written by a "Ph.D. candidate at the Chinese People's University," and dated May 1, 1989, the complete title of this piece ends with, "a comparative analysis that the authorities try desperately to avoid."

12. Produced by an anonymous author from Beijing Normal University.

13. We should remember here that during the previous ten years economic reforms had permitted a significant private sector to develop within the Chinese system of state socialism.

14. The name is probably a pseudonym. At the beginning of the document was the statement, "The author is a student in the Chinese Department, lacking in theoretical sophistication, and would be grateful to hear the views of others in response to his own."

15. This piece appeared on the Beijing University campus, May 17, 1989.

16. A student, writing before the massacre.

17. Ma, aged 25 at the time of the May 13th-20th hunger strike, had left school eight years earlier. He had followed various professions, including those of editor, free-lance writer, reporter, employee in a cultural bureau, and accountant. In 1986 he had been admitted to the Beijing Cinema College, taking the Literature Editing programme.
18. Prominent figure in the Student Movement.
19. This is an interesting play upon an old theme. Mao Zedong had said that the revolutionary guerrilla fighters are fish, and the people are the water in which they swim, and which they need to survive. Now, the people are seen as the fish, but the communist party is presented as a net restraining and destroying them.
20. Former director of the Institute of Marxism-Leninism-Mao Zedong Thought of the Chinese Academy of Social Sciences, dismissed during the "anti-bourgeois liberalization" campaign of 1987, and today a political exile in the U.S.A.
21. In an otherwise coherent analysis of the economic variables involved in the 1989 events, this view, that the Movement was linked with an emerging bourgeoisie, is unpersuasive. The reader will note that students and workers were the core of the Movement, and the documents in this volume are representative of that fact. Furthermore, the demands are most obviously egalitarian and communitarian. Analytical speculations of the kind that Su Shaozhi gives here, unwarranted by any facts, are the sort of thing that made Wuer Kaixi, a leading spokesman of the students, reject the intellectuals (see Section Four of this volume). Such views also imply that revolutions in "socialist States" have a single option, which is capitalism — a denial of alternatives which strips the Movement of its entire radical character.

II

CHINESE SOCIETY OPPOSES THE STATE
Pamphlets and Wall Posters [1]

STUDENT COMMENT

XIII: The Shortcomings of the Stalinist Political System

The fundamental shortcoming of all socialist countries is a political system that replaces the people with bureaucrats as the masters of society. The leader enjoys life-long tenure of office with enough power even to appoint his own successor. Such a practice runs counter to the principles of a republic, and carries rather the characteristics of a monarchical autocracy. That is why socialist countries are republics in name only, and monarchies in reality. China is no exception. Our socialism has been a feudalistic socialism, which is the socialism of the Stalinist Model. Stalin was a typical tyrant whose regime was a proletarian or socialist monarchy; and that of Mao Zedong was of the same kind.

The shortcomings of this political structure are,

1) concentration of the power of the leadership,
2) life-long tenure of office,
3) leadership choice of the successor,
4) the unity of party and government, and
5) high-ranking cadres are concerned only with gaining privileges.

With this in mind, I think that our most immediate task is to carry through a political reform with speed and determination.

April 25, 1989

XIV: An Outline of the Communist Party

The party leader: The party chief, lionized, and treated like a god in a movement tied to traditional Chinese culture, is alienated from the people. Egocentricity and the autocracy in turn make him into a dictator.

The party cadres: Humble servants of the patriarchal party chief and the arrogant *nouveaux riches.* They demand the subservience of the people, abuse their privileges and power for personal gain, and corrupt the legal system.

The party organization: A hierarchy of gangsters, riddled with factional struggles, whilst eradicating any non-party opposition.

The quality of the party: 75% of this 47,000,000-strong "vanguard" have received only a primary school education.

Party membership: A pragmatic act for the acquisition of a party card. Presenting the image of progressiveness, but being the means of extortion for personal gain, party membership creates a bunch of schizophrenic hypocrites, whatever their original characters. This seriously influences the consciousness of the people, inhibiting their development.

The behaviour of the party: Irrefutable sacred order and empty dogmas allow the leader to initiate "cultural revolutions" and "rectification campaigns" that threaten the survival of the nation, whilst causing widespread suffering and death. Under cover of these orders and dogmas, the cadres deceive the people, making dirty deals in the shadow of their sacred banner.

The Party's Four Modernizations:

1) idolization of the party's image,
2) unending justification of the party's role,
3) intensification of its power and privileges, and
4) the corruption of the party cadres.

The CCP: Omnipotent Leviathan, God Almighty, to whom the people must bow. The party leader gives orders to start the machine, the cadres and party members[2] act as cogs. So many of the best of our race have been strangled by this machine.

The greatness of the party: "She can correct her mistakes."

Blood might cleanse the shame of the autocracy, and breed a generation of genuine communists; but it can also be the breeding ground for a new sect of the rich and the powerful, as well as a new dictator.

[undated]

XV: *Who Causes the Turmoil?*

The great Student Movement has been called a "turmoil" deliberately manufactured by the students. However, any thinking person can see that this is an attempt at distortion and deception. Who does not know that the corrupt and incompetent government is the creator of the widespread, patriotic "turmoil"?

A peaceful Movement which organises a petition is no bad thing for an enlightened government. From the very start, however, the government adopted an indifferent attitude to the students, responding only after it became too large to ignore. And their response was to use their control of the media to point an accusing finger and shout, "Turmoil." Thus did turmoil begin.

We were all small children during the Great Cultural Revolution, and we do not know much about it. The voices of officialdom remember it, however, and use the language of that time. They speak of "a small minority," with "ulterior motives," in "a conspiracy long concocted." It sounds so frightening, and so silly, as they try to take China back to the days of the Cultural Revolution. Let us, the students and masses, respond by accusing *them* of being the real "small minority, with ulterior motives," and tell them that we will not allow *their* "long-concocted conspiracy" to succeed!

It is true that stability and solidarity are conducive to development. However, remember that a docile population provides huge opportunities for those who would exploit the masses. Therefore, we must not continue to be passive. We must eliminate the termites of reforms and the parasites of development. Only then will China be able to develop in healthy stability and solidarity.

Of course, a country's leaders cannot be ever available "on demand." However, could they please let us know under what circumstances they will meet with the people. More than one hundred thousand are asking for a meeting with the leaders on matters of life and death for the nation. Is that not enough?

China's democratization must proceed. History has seen nothing like what is happening today, and as history the experience is important. All righteous compatriots, including open-minded officials in high positions, think seriously about it with us!

April 28, 1989

XVI: *Talking with Two Workers*[3]

I did not have much understanding of the Student Movement, and did not join in the demonstrations of April 20th and April 22nd. What has happened since then, however, has left me very disturbed, and I have decided to join the organization of patriotic students and be more than a spectator of revolution.

I was one of the participants in the demonstration of April 27th, the character of which requires no further description. Here I would like to describe a conversation that I had with two workers at noon today, showing thereby the views and hopes of the citizens in relation to our movement.

The two workers were from different enterprises, and both were university graduates. One of them had resigned from his government position and had opened two cafes. The other was a worker in a research unit. Our main topic of discussion is summarised in the following statement by the latter: "The Student Movement has gained the support of the citizens and the workers." To prove this he told me how the workers of his unit responded to the editorial in the *People's Daily*. The workers asked a lot of awkward questions, and complained about unequal rewards, long working hours, poor social welfare, and lack of protection of workers' right to an education, etc. A low ranking party official, listening to them, replied sarcastically that everyone has problems.

One of the workers told me that he went to the meat store to buy some ribs, and was told, "the ribs are reserved for the university students." The customers supported this. He also said that if students went to enterprises for donations, they would get anything they needed. The workers are waiting for our requests.

Fellow students, your actions are recognised by society, people support you and want you to carry on. The government has already lost the support of the people. If the students lose a single drop of blood in the fight, the workers in the city will unite in a protest strike against the government.

Finally, the workers repeatedly asked me to pass on the good will of the workers to the active students. They want to hear more of our theories, and to be made aware of the government's deviousness.

When we said goodbye they made the "V" sign, and also clenched their fists and shouted, "The people appreciate you, and history will remember you. Struggle on obstinately. Victory belongs to you and to the people."

April 29, 1989

XVII: A Short Commentary on the Slogan, "Down with the Communist Party" [4]

The state radio has been saying that the slogan, "Down with the Communist Party," was heard during the April 20th demonstration.

If it were shouted, and by whom, is not my concern here. What does the slogan itself reflect? That is more to the point.

When Sun Yatsen founded the Nationalist Party [Guomintang] at the time of the national revolution [1911], that party was undoubtedly the vanguard of its time and, therefore, well received by the people. Even founder members of the CCP, like Li Dazhou, Mao Zedong and Zhou Enlai, were members of the Nationalist Party for a time. The slogan, "Down with the Nationalist Party," was surely counter-revolutionary then. With the passing of time, however, and the degeneration of the Nationalist Party, things changed. During the Great Revolutionary and Anti-Japanese War [1936-1945] and the Liberation War [1945-1949] period, the Nationalist Party was opposed to the historical trend. It wanted a one-party, one-man dictatorship in China. The people responded with the slogan, "Down with the Nationalist reactionaries" and, "Overthrow the feudalistic regime of Chiang Kaishek." Such slogans were undoubtedly the general will of the progressive forces and historically correct.

The process through which the Nationalist Party moved from a progressive to a reactionary position illustrates a general Marxist truth: when a party (or its leaders) cease to represent the people as a whole, it will be forsaken by history.

In the late eighties of the twentieth century the People's Republic of China is in its middle years. We are confused when we awake to find ourselves a member of the international community, and ask, "What has the CCP achieved during the past forty years?" Living standards have certainly improved, but there is reason for concern. Information in student pamphlets, and the violent response of the government, must lead us to the conclusion that we are building on foundations of sand.

What does the slogan, "Down with the CCP," imply?

If the CCP still represents the people, let me suggest the following:

1) If the slogan was shouted ask, "By whom?"
2) If it was shouted by the "enemy," ignore it. Our one billion people will scotch the rumour, no matter how vicious it is.
3) If it is the people who are shouting, we should take it as an alarm signal.
4) Fear is a sign of a lack of courage, which produces a lack of confidence.

I believe in the communist blueprint outlined by Marx. I will firmly support a CCP that represents the interests of the people.

April 30, 1989

XVIII: The Ten Differences Between the Patriotic Movement and the Cultural Revolution[5]

	THE PRESENT MOVEMENT	THE CULTURAL REVOLUTION
Nature	Opposed to remnants of feudalism, anti-bureaucratic; for science, democracy and freedom.	Strengthened the personality cult and placed one billion people in intellectual bondage.
Basic Character	Awakening the people.	Serious turmoil.
Goal	To quicken the pace for democratic form.	To protect the bureaucracy and the party.
Results	Ideas of democracy have been embedded in the minds of the people. Support for reform.	No progressive results. Major historical retrogression.
Initiation	Spontaneous organization of students.	Chairman Mao alone.
Methods	Non-violent petitions, constitutional.	Violence, arson, robbery and lawlessness.
Means	Strikes, demonstrations and requests for dialogue.	The more confusion the better, the whole country paralysed.
Attitude towards CCP	Supporting correct leadership and opposing corruption therein.	Making revolution by destroying party committees, autocratic rule by the head of a sect.
Response of the masses	Respect for the masses produces widespread support and sympathy.	The hoodwinked masses groan.
Its place in history	Of equal importance to May Fourth Movement.	Eternally despised!

April 30, 1989

XIX: The Patriotic-Democratic Movement Compared with the Turmoil of the Cultural Revolution[6]

The *People's Daily* editorial of April 26, 1989, described the current Democratic-Patriotic Movement as an anti-party cause of turmoil. It attempted to liken it to the turmoil experienced during the decade of the Cultural Revolution. Moreover, when students and government officials met on April 29th, Yuan Mu stated that the two were similar. From the perspective of this writer, however, there are great differences, as the present analysis will show to the reader.

Considering the background of the two disruptions:

1) The ten years of turmoil were initiated, wrongly, by a faction of the party to promote its interest in factional struggles by upholding the personality cult. The present Movement is the consummation of the whole complex of social contradictions. It is the spontaneous product of a society in a state of crisis, and has the purpose of accelerating the democratization of China, promoting political reform, fighting official corruption, and eliminating decadence, so that intellectuals, workers and peasants can benefit from reforms in a richer and stronger nation. Nobody with "ulterior motives" is making use of the movement!

2) The Cultural Revolution remained under the influence of the personality cult, with the main force of the rebellion, the masses and the Red Guards, ignorant and easily misled. This made its manipulation inevitable. The current Movement, on the other hand, came into being after China had experienced ten years of reform. The mass of young students and intellectuals have studied and learned from western liberal-democratic ideas, have made a special analysis of the Chinese situation, and have suggested a series of political and economic reforms. Formulating ideas on democracy and freedom, intellectuals, students, workers and ordinary citizens from the different economic strata, have clearly organised their thoughts in order to fight for democracy, freedom, prosperity and the future strength of China. They are certainly not used by anyone with "ulterior motives." They have brains, and their IQs are certainly no lower than those of the bureaucrats!

3) During the ten years of turmoil sects and factions flourished. The present Movement, however, goes to the people not to form factions but to arouse them as a whole, and to enlighten them with democratic ideas for the early implementation of a democratic system. One must go to the people to achieve the realization of freedom of speech.

Concerning contradictions in the CCP, we may also note:

4) During the Cultural Revolution some people made revolution simply to get rid of the local party committee and satisfy their own greed for power in their schools, departments, factories, mines, etc. The present Movement, however, stands for the correct leadership of the CCP. We are demanding that the party not abuse its power in society, and desist from intervention in normal administrative matters. We are definitely not opposed to the proper leadership of the CCP, and are trying to promote that through a separation of party and government. Those who attack us for being anti-party have ulterior motives. We must not permit anyone, using the excuse of the Four Cardinal Principles, to muddy the issue.

Concerning the consequences of the two situations:

5) The ten years of turmoil brought great disasters to the nation, involving the persecution of intellectuals, damage to democracy and the legal system, taking the economy to the verge of collapse, and disrupting the education system. The present Democratic-Patriotic Movement will lead eventually to the strengthening of the democratic system and rule of law. The masses will have greater democracy and freedom. Government officials will be honest. Education will benefit. The Chinese nation will prosper!

In sum, and taking into consideration the participants in the two movements, the present one differs greatly from the ten years of turmoil. One hopes that people can see the difference between right and wrong. We must not let government officials make false linkages and accusations, and destroy the solidarity of the students, intellectuals, workers and peasants. We must not allow the government bureaucrats to use this pretext to suppress the students' Democratic-Patriotic Movement. We must unite and fight for our common democratic goals!

May 3, 1989

XX: For the Democracy Fighters [7]

Nearly three years ago I experienced the end of the Shanghai Movement with a sense of hopelessness. However, as a person with that experience, and as a sympathizer, there is much that I can say to you.

This movement surpasses the earlier one in both its size and the range of its activities. However, the response of the authorities is exactly the same. One cannot help thinking that the end will be the same.

In Shanghai the students first marched, then organised a sit-in strike. The authorities resorted to the guerrilla tactic of "hitting when the enemy is tired," using the military and police to disperse the students when they were at their weakest. The basic move of the authorities is the human wall tactic, sending a mass of soldiers and police to confront the students face to face. How could under-nourished students compete? So, regretfully, they had to back down, and the armed forces were victorious. Then, as now, we thought that we held an advantage; but look what happened.

In 1986 in Shanghai, after a week of marches, demonstrations and sit-ins, we began a general strike in the institutions of higher education on December 24th. We held theoretical discussions, seeking to give direction to the movement. We were optimistic. On the evening of December 31st, at an open forum at the university, the mood was jubilant and victory was proclaimed. Nobody anticipated that on the following morning, the first document of the new year totally reversed the situation. Serious matters became small matters, which then became irrelevant. That is the entire story. The revolution was aborted.

Here in Beijing the participants in the current Movement realise the need for theoretical direction. A leadership has been organised, think-tanks are in operation. I am encouraged by this, and hope that the lessons of 1986 will enable us to formulate a victorious policy for the Democracy Movement. In so doing, I recommend the following:

The success or failure of the Movement will hinge on a resolute leadership and the willingness of some members of the Movement to sacrifice themselves. Students have mixed feelings. Some see the Movement as the opportunity of a lifetime; and to be involved is, of course, more exciting than the boredom of lectures and academic work. Others regard the struggle for democracy as a holy task. Yet, compared with the May Fourth Movement our modern activists are faced with many more difficulties. Success or failure, as in 1986, will depend upon a willingness to face the authorities, "not shying away from bloody incidents." That should be our greatest concern.

[undated]

XXI: *Statement of the May 13th Hunger Strikers*

We commence our hunger strike in the lovely May sunshine. In the full bloom of youth, however, we leave beautiful things behind, but with great reluctance.

Yet the condition of our country is one of rampant inflation, economic speculation by officials, extreme authoritarian rule, serious bureaucratic corruption, a drain of products and people to other countries, social confusion and an increase in the number of criminal acts. It is a crucial moment for the country and its people. All compatriots with a conscience, please heed our call:

The country is our country.
The people are our people.
The government is our government.
If we do not cry out, who will?
If we do not take action, who will?

Our bodies are still tender and not full grown, and the prospect of dying frightens us all; but history calls us and we must go.

Our purest and patriotic love, and our most generous sentiments, have been called a "turmoil" with "ulterior motives," which is "manipulated by a handful of people."

We ask every Chinese citizen with a sense of justice, every worker, peasant, soldier, intellectual, celebrity, government official, policeman and even our accusers, to look into their hearts and ask what crime has been committed. Is it a "rebellion" to strike, to demonstrate, and to go on a hunger strike? Why must we hide ourselves away? Our feelings have been treated too lightly. We live in miserable conditions as we search for truth, and then are beaten up by the police. Student representatives kneel to request democracy, and are ignored. Our request for an equal dialogue is repeatedly ignored, and the student leaders are put in a very dangerous position.

What shall we do?

Democracy is a desire intrinsic to the human condition. Freedom is an inherent human right. We now must sacrifice our lives for them. Is this something that the Chinese race should be proud of?

The hunger strike was forced upon us as a last resort. We face death resolutely, although we are fighting for life. We are still very young. China, our mother! Look closely at your sons and daughters. Hunger is ravaging their youth and death is near. Can you stand unmoved?

We do not want to die. We have a passionate desire to live on in the prime of our lives. We want to live and to learn. Our motherland is poor, and we do not want to leave her so. No, we are not seeking death; but if death could lead to improved conditions and prosperity for our country, then we ought not shun it.

Though we are starving, dear parents, do not despair. When we bid farewell to life, dear uncles and aunts, do not be unhappy. We hope only that you will live better. Remember always that we were not looking for death, and that democracy is not the product of a few, nor the accomplishment of a single generation.

Death awaits. Farewell. To our colleagues who share our loyalties. To our loved ones, whom we would rather not leave, but whom we must. To our mothers and fathers, for whom we cannot be both patriotic and filial at the same time. To the people of our country, from whom we ask permission to pursue this final act of loyalty.

We make a commitment with our lives, to make the sky of the republic clear and bright.

Reasons for the Hunger Strike:

First, to protest against the casual attitude of the government towards the demonstration of the Beijing students. Second, to protest the government's continued refusal to engage in a dialogue with the representatives of Beijing's institutions of higher education. Third, to protest against the government's condemnation of the patriotic movement as "turmoil," and the distortions of the media.

Demands of the Hunger Strikers:
First, that the government quickly enter into equal, concrete discussion with the Dialogue Group of the Beijing institutions of higher education. Second, that the government retract its statements concerning the nature of the Student Movement, and evaluate it fairly and honestly as a patriotic and democratic Movement.

May 13, 1989

XXII: A Declaration of Emergency to all the People of the Country from the People of the Capital

The capital is in danger! China is in danger! The nation is in danger! The People's Republic is in fatal danger.

Faced with the recent struggle for democracy by thousands of patriotic students and citizens, the ruling group destabilized the situation by declaring martial law, and defining the widely supported and great Patriotic Movement as "turmoil." This is an outright denial of the republic's Constitution. They go totally against the people, becoming their oppressors, and are therefore traitors and enemies of the republic. They cannot be representing the party and the country.

Now is the darkest, bloodiest, most inhuman and disappointing moment of the republic's history. The republic faces a most difficult task as a "Tiananmen Incident" again occurs. The situation becomes totalitarian, cruel, dictatorial and bloody.

In this serious situation, we call upon the several hundred thousand students, and ten million citizens, are urgently called upon to make a general strike. Vast quantities of propaganda are also directed at the People's Liberation Army, asking them to stand alongside the people, and refuse to become the weapons of a bloody crackdown by the governing group.

That group is prepared to kill. In this emergency they have openly trampled on the Constitution, openly become an enemy of the republic, and openly betrayed their responsibilities as members of the Standing Committee of the National People's Congress. Therefore, we must struggle to enforce the collective resignation of the ruling group. They must openly confess their crimes, and their political actions must be investigated. This is the only acceptable choice.

The population of the capital opposes bloody repression and terror, and is mentally prepared to fight to the end. Now that it is mobilised and prepared for conflict, we say to the whole country:

1) Start a "national non-cooperation movement" against the government. The ruling group does not represent the country, and its instructions can be ignored.

2) Begin countrywide support activities, especially in relation to the provision of medical and first-aid supplies.

3) Start a petition for all elected People's Representatives [to the National People's Congress] demanding the resignation of [President] Yang Shangkun, [Vice-President] Wang Zhen, [Premier] Li peng, and [Vice-Premier] Yao Yilin, who must be removed to avoid widespread bloodshed and save the republic.

4) Urgently demand the various armies [of the PLA] to stand by the people, protect the people, and punish the political criminals.

5) Demand of the governments in the provinces, cities, autonomous areas and military areas, that they support the people of the capital, condemn the ruling group, protect administrative stability, object to the use of military force, and openly state that militarism is the character of the central government.

6) Urgently appeal for the support of all governments and peoples of the world.

7) Urgently appeal to all people for an unyielding struggle with the anti-democratic and anti-revolutionary group of Yang, Wang, Li and Yao. It is they who have become the main representatives of power corruption, and who, by means of an anti-revolutionary military coup, have stolen the supreme power of the party and the country, betraying the National People's Congress and its Standing Committee.

8) Everyone must rescue China from this danger. We must begin to develop a new republican order, following the example of the new generation. To do this great thing, victory must go to the people.

9) The current military government must be held responsible for the bloodshed and repression that is about to occur. The united strength of the people must punish them for these crimes through the highest legal channels.

10) The population of the capital and all patriotic students have determined to protect the republic, and the dignity of the Constitution, with their freedom, their blood and their lives, risking all in the fight.

Everyone must unite! The people must win! Long live the people's Democracy Movement!

May 20, 1989

XXIII: A Statement for Citizens Concerning the Army Entering the Capital

To all citizens and comrades:

The Patriotic-Democracy Movement has lasted for more than one month, during which time you have actively participated and contributed to the national well-being. Of late, people in the central government have destroyed the honour of both the party and the government. They have lied to the soldiers of the PLA as they seek to suppress the people with bloody violence. In these circumstances we appeal to everyone to stop the army from entering the city, doing so with reference to the following points:

1) The soldiers are not our real enemies, but our brothers. They are lied to, and do not know the real situation. Some of them are not now permitted to read newspapers or watch television. Therefore, tell them the true story, inform them of our intentions, using persuasion rather than force, and thereby gaining their understanding and respect.

2) An irresponsible and dishonest government, which has lied to the soldiers, is also providing inadequate rations for them, in order to increase the tension between them and the people. Consequently, we must care for the soldiers, and help them to solve their food problems.

3) We must recognise that soldiers must obey orders, but we must let them know that they can refuse orders which go against the people. We must block them, but avoid conflict with them; and remain aware that policemen in civilian clothes and others with bad intentions might attack soldiers in order to increase tensions.

4) If the army wish to retreat, permit them to do so.

May 20, 1989

XXIV: A Statement for the Soldiers[8]

Greetings to all soldiers in the People's Liberation Army!

Before everything else, please remember that you are the army of the people and the country, responsible for the protection of their welfare. Know also that the real reason for your entering the capital is to repress the people. However, the people here believe in you, and ask you to look at the real nature of things.

You will see clearly that people are suffering, that the future of our nation lies in your support for the university students, some of whom have been on hunger strike for seven days. Everyone is worried about them, trying to help them. The police have disappeared, and volunteer pickets are spontaneously organising the movement of traffic. So why does the government continue to ignore our two minimum requests (i.e., withdraw the April 26th *People's Daily* editorial and hold a dialogue with the students, to be broadcast live)? Several thousand students, 3000 of whom have already fainted, are on hunger strike in support of these two demands. They are met with weapons.

We speak with the voice of the people, and want to replace economic manipulation and corruption by the bureaucracy with democracy and legality. What is wrong with that? The demonstration by a million people in Beijing, and the petitioning of the students, are systematically organised with cool-headed and rational restraint. There has been no disastrous incident. So the government delay is contradictory. Instead of saying, "There is no government," we should be asking, "Where is the government?"

Then out comes the government at last, after a struggle within the hierarchy. There is no turmoil here. They are using you, soldiers and brothers, to suppress the people in the interests of those few people.

Soldiers! We love you, and your hands must not be stained with the people's blood. Facing you there are starving students supported by millions of people. On this day dictators have attempted to cheat the people, and as such will their names live in history!

In the last analysis, history is written by the people!

Soldiers and brothers, please think again, and do not violate the hopes of the people. Think carefully about your own families!

May 21, 1989

XXV: The Most Dangerous Emergency

The current situation gives cause for widespread concern. Martial law has been declared, and soldiers summoned to Beijing. These soldiers are sons and brothers of the people, nurtured by them. The army and the country rise and fall together. When the country is in danger, it is there to protect the people. With the people in jeopardy, the soldiers will protect them, not harm them. We believe that they will make a reasonable choice on the matter of martial law. The people's wishes cannot be countermanded by a small group with special powers. Denied information for a month, our soldiers must now be told the truth, that they may unite with us in the promotion of the Patriotic-Democracy Movement, for total victory.

XXVI: An Open Letter to our Brothers, the Soldiers[9]

For six days the patriotic students have been on a hunger strike; and what has been the result? Their petition and actions have been described as turmoil, and in need of repression. How rational is that? And why should we agree with those in power?

When the students began their hunger strike on May 13th, the government was unsympathetic, and resorted to removing the police who control the traffic [in the square], and refusing to meet with them. These are cunning and underhand tactics.

Soldiers of the People's Liberation Army, sons and brothers of the people, remember that the people are not slaves, and that they love the soldiers. Join with the people to defeat totalitarianism and promote democracy in China!

The sleeping lion has wakened! There is hope for China!

Dated, "one morning in May."

XXVII: An Open Letter to all Soldiers in the People's Liberation Army

To all soldiers in the Liberation Army:

From mid-April, in Beijing and throughout the country, thousands of students have held rallies, written big character posters, held study strikes and hunger strikes. They have urged the government to get rid of corruption, abuse of power, black-marketeering bureaucrats, inflation and other problems. In the last few days newspapers, radio, and television have been reporting these facts. Why have you not been allowed to know it? Is the government afraid to let you know the truth, and that workers and farmers generally support the students, providing food and drink for them. In the last few days the people of the capital have gone onto the streets in support of the hunger strikers, including many people from central government organizations, the *People's Daily*, Central Party School, the central radio, departments of the State Council, and even policemen and soldiers.

Soldiers of the army, you are brothers of workers, farmers, and citizens from all strata of society. The Patriotic-Democratic Movement, begun by the students, demands rights for the people. The students have made great sacrifices for all of the people. For eight days thousands of them have been on hunger strike, two thousand have lost consciousness, many might die. All generous people think that the government is conscientious, but is ignoring the people, rejecting the two reasonable requests of the students: i) to admit that the Student Movement is a Movement, and ii) to meet the students for equal dialogue. On the contrary, it sends you to suppress them, treating you as a mindless tool, pursuing its ends by having the people kill each other.

Soldiers! The people understand your situation. Our common goals, however, are destroying corruption and fighting for democracy. The 38th Army has refused the order to suppress the students, and have retreated from Beijing. What would you do?

The whole country is watching you! We hope that you will not do anything to break our fraternal hearts!

May 21, 1989

XXVIII: A Statement to All Soldiers [10]

Dear Soldiers of the Liberation Army,

The PLA is made up of the sons and brothers of the people. You guard and protect the republic, not just a small minority. In a life or death situation you should look closely at the wishes of the people, and not become the tool of their repression at the orders of one or a few.

In the development of the Patriotic-Democracy Movement you have supported the people in your own way. The soldiers of the 38th Army have refused to obey the illegal order to suppress the people, and are thereby the brilliant representatives of the people, who welcome them. [11]

Stand with the people! Protect the Constitution! Maintain democracy and reform!

May 21, 1989

XXIX: To the Workers' Picket Group [12]

All workers, citizens, and comrades,

Thank you for your hard work. For more than a month you have given your support to this great Patriotic Movement, both materially and spiritually. The patriotic students have spoken for you, and we have strong linkages. When we marched through the streets, you clapped and cheered for us, gave us food and water, and unselfishly supported us. When we protested against the government's shameful actions, you gave us passionate support, without which we could never have lasted. Honest people, you are usually quite ordinary; but you gave tremendous strength at a critical time. Before you, all other powers are comparatively small and pitiful.

The pitiful and pathetic Li Peng, whose hypocritical government did not respond to the legitimate demands of the students, even falsely accused the Student Movement of fomenting a riot, using this as an excuse to order troops into Beijing. They said that the troops are needed to keep the peace, when in fact they are for a brutal crackdown. The Patriotic Movement is about to be destroyed, and you have stood by our side, bravely preventing the troops from entering Beijing. Today is the eighth day of martial law, and this hypocritical government has vulgarly and treacherously organised something called the workers' picket group, helping the troops enter Beijing. But don't think that workers and students are going to fight each other for the benefit of the government. There is a rumour that plainclothes police have infiltrated the workers' picket group as agitators with evil designs. Workers, citizens, and compatriots, keep your eyes open. We believe, however, that, even if there are police among you, as Chinese with a conscience they will not help Li Peng clear the streets in opposition to democracy and the people.

If the government acted honestly they would get more support. The Li Peng government, however, in its final struggles, dishonest, cannot last much longer.

Workers, farmers, soldiers, students and businessmen, unite to fight for democracy in the People's Republic of China.

May 28, 1989

XXX: Who Created the Turmoils of the Last Forty Years?

In 1957 Mao Zedong waged an anti-rightist struggle in which millions of intellectuals were condemned. Many were imprisoned and exiled, whilst countless others were forced into suicide.

From 1958 to 1962 Mao promoted the Great Leap Forward, which produced an unprecedented decline in the national economy. Countless numbers died of starvation. Everywhere people suffered from illness and malnutrition.

From 1966 to 1976 Mao Zedong pursued the Great Cultural Revolution, which brought disaster to the whole nation.

During 1983 and 1984 Deng Xiaoping promoted the national campaign to eliminate criminal elements. Many people were falsely accused, and a widespread criticism of the campaign developed.

In 1987 Deng Xiaoping initiated the campaign against bourgeois liberalism. This generated serious confusion in ideas and ideology, and led to the resignation of Hu Yaobang and the exile of many intellectuals. It was also a barrier to scientific and cultural progress.

From July to October, 1988, serious inflation was produced by poor central economic decisions. Panic buying occurred as people emptied their bank accounts.

On May 20, 1989, Deng Xiaoping, Li Peng, and Yang Shangkun assaulted public opinion and established military law in Beijing. Hundreds of thousands of armed soldiers were sent to suppress the masses. Huge opposition to this move came from the students and people of Beijing, who sought to keep out the troops. They were supported by the people of all of China, of the whole world.

Experience demonstrates that none of the turmoil since the beginning of the people's republic [1949] has been created by democratic parties — nor by the people, nor by the USA, nor Taiwan, nor the USSR. It has been caused by a small group of people in the Political Bureau of the CCP, who have usurped power over the party, the government, and the armed forces.

[undated]

XXXI: What do Factional Disputes Reveal? [13]

The abnormal phenomena occurring in the contemporary political scene lead us to think that there are factional disputes occurring within the government. What these disputes reveal is of some concern.

Our party's history is riddled with factional disputes. From Chen Duxiu,[14] Zhang Guodao,[15] Wang Ming[16] to Liu, Deng and Zhou,[17] and the Jiang Qing — Lin Biao clique;[18] and it continues today, the scars of the past being no guarantee against new wounds today. These scars are a record of the great price paid by the people and the party, being evidence in particular of a lack of democracy in the CCP.

The supposed infallibility of Mao Zedong in the revolutionary struggle created in the people a psychological dependence, incapable of defending one's position, of surviving, without the powerful leader. Under a spell like that, people lose their ability to think critically and independently. All they can do is swear allegiance to whoever is in power, whilst allowing those who possess authority to consolidate power; and that is the source of factions.

Factional struggles can only be avoided if people in power respect democratic procedures. Without democratic structures no party organization can develop a common goal. Rules and regulations which are supposed to generate unity must be a sham, and crises are inevitable. This is particularly true in the context of the traditional culture of our bureaucracy, whereby the sole end of knowledge is to pass the official examination for the recruitment of government officials. Officials tend to desire power in this environment. Coups are almost inevitable, as the experience of our party painfully demonstrates. Some of them may be necessary, but the political circumstances generating them are not healthy. Genuine democracy in the party is the only way to eliminate the problem.

Without democracy, factional disputes are inevitable, and one-man rule will remain. The serious consequences will be exhaustion and chaos everywhere, as can be seen in our country. The struggle for genuine democracy is, therefore, a struggle against factions, and a commitment by the people to the strengthening of the whole of China.

Long live democracy! Long live the people!

May 25, 1989

RESPONSE OF THE WORKERS

XXXII: Letter to the People of Beijing (BWU) [19]

The entire population of China must now face up to an intolerable situation. Long accustomed to bureaucratic-dictatorial forms of control, they must now live with uncontrolled inflation and declining living standards. To recover from their extravagant behaviour, the ruling elite have issued various government and treasury bonds, squeezing the people for every penny of their cash. In this situation, people from all walks of life must join together to reveal the truth and protect the future of China.

Those of us who are policemen and soldiers must stand by the people, for truth, not serve as tools of the people's enemies. You are also being oppressed. As for the murderers in the April Fifth Incident and the April Twentieth Bloodshed [of 1976], the people will never forget your crimes.

We earnestly demand the following: a wage increase, price stabilization, and a publication of the incomes and possessions of government officials and their families. We, the workers of Beijing, and citizens from all walks of life, support the university students and their fight for honesty and justice.

April 20, 1989.

XXXIII: Ten Polite Questions for the CCP (BWU):

1) How much did Deng's son bet on a horse race in Hong Kong, and where did he get the money to place the bet?

2) Mr. and Mrs. Zhao Ziyang play golf every week. Who pays the green fees, and other expenses?

3) How does the Central Committee [of the CCP] judge the ongoing reforms. In his New Year Address Premier Li Peng said that there have been mistakes. What are they? What exactly is the situation now?

4) The Central Committee has proposed a reform for the control of prices, yet inflation continues, with the people's living standard declining. Can they explain this?

5) China must begin the repayment of foreign loans in 1990. How much must each citizen contribute to this? Will it affect basic living standards? Please answer us.

6) Deng Xiaoping has suggested raising the status of intellectuals from "stinking ninth" to "top rank." [20] What is a top ranking person? Would that be a landlord? Or a landlord's father?

7) How many residences and retreats do top party officials have spread around the country? What do they cost? Can this be made public? Please answer us.

8) Make public the personal incomes and possessions of top party officials.

9) How is the party going to respond to approaches from the government of Taiwan for peace talks?

10) Would the party be so kind as to explain the meaning and implications of the following terms: i) Party, ii) Revolution, and iii) Reactionary.

Would the party please publish their responses to the above ten questions as soon as possible?

April 20, 1989,

XXXIV: Letter to Compatriots of the Nation (BWU)

The illegal behaviour of the corrupt officials has reached the extreme! The brutality of officials reaches the extreme! In a vast country like China, there is no place for truth! No repression can stop the people's anger; no longer will people believe the lies of the government; and the words on our standard are: science, democracy, freedom, human rights, laws and institutions!

The Beijing Workers' Union was established on April 20th to protect the rights of workers; and we published our "Letter" to the people of the city and "Ten Questions." The April 26th editorial falsely stated that these documents were counter-revolutionary. We must request that, in the absence of any answers to our ten questions, that you publish the two documents in your newspaper. Or are you too much afraid, even after parading the slogan, "Believe in the People," for the past forty years? We demand a retraction of the April 26th editorial comment, and the punishment of its author and party sponsors.

We have carefully considered the exploitation of the workers. Marx's *Capital* provided us with a method for understanding the character of our oppression. We deducted from the total value of output the workers wages, welfare, medical welfare, the necessary social fund, equipment depreciation and reinvestment expenses. Surprisingly, we discovered that "civil servants" swallow all the remaining value produced by the people's blood and sweat! The total taken by them is really vast! How cruel! How typically Chinese! These bureaucrats use the people's hard earned money to build luxury villas all over the country (guarded by soldiers in so-called military areas), to buy luxury cars, to travel to foreign countries on so-called study tours (with their families, and even baby sitters)! Their immoral and shameful deeds and crimes are too numerous to mention here.

Concerning the general welfare, Comrade Fang Lizhi's views on the subject of off-shore investment is true. Foreign investment eventually becomes the legal property of top officials, through *Guandao* (i.e., bureaucratic corruption). The victim is the country, the beneficiaries are a small minority, and the people pay for it.

We strongly protest the savage action of forcing the people to buy treasury bonds. We demand that the government provide a report on income and expenditure in this trade, return the money with interest to the bond holders, and close the bond markets which are a main source of income for *Guandao*. We demand an increase in wages, the stabilization of inflation, an end to the refusal to adjust wages according to age and experience. We demand the investigation of the top party officials of the CCP Central Committee's Central Advisory Commission, the Central Committee itself, the Politburo, the Central Military Commission of the CCP. The first to be investigated should be those who have luxury villas; like Deng Xiaoping, Zhao Ziyang, Li Peng, Chen Yun, Li Xiannian, Yang Shangkun, Peng Zhen, and Jiang Zemin,[21] and their families. This should be done by a "national investigation committee," elected by the people, and reporting to them.

The students are now responsible, the good discipline of their several millions in Tiananmen Square being ample proof. The people have awakened! They understand that, whatever the society, whatever the moment in history, there are only two classes, those who rule and those who are ruled. Viewing the history of the party, the society, and the individual, we see revolutionary progress starting with the overthrow of the Qing dynasty [1910]. However, it has to this point been change which is "ruled by man." That is why the Chinese still love, need, praise and remember the "honest official." The political movement in these past forty years, however, has been a political suppression of the people. History is showing that they are good at an "appraisal after autumn" [i.e., seeing their mistakes when it is too late to correct them]; and they cannot change history.

Those politicians who are using the Democracy Movement of the students should take heed. Deng made use of the April Fifth Movement to become leader of the party, and has demonstrated the awful consequences. The economic reforms which followed are both superficial and fake. The standard of living has declined for most people, and heavy debts remain to be paid by the people.

Workers. Comrades. Keep closely united to the Beijing Workers' Union. Under its direction the democratic movement should be pushed to a new climax. Our union is going to hold a workers' march to Tiananmen Square on May 22nd at 2:00 p.m., to demonstrate peacefully and support the university students. The slogan is, "In a vast country like China, there is not even a place for truth!"

May 17, 1989

XXXV: Letter to the Students [22]

Dear Students,

As you continue your struggle over the following days you must try to gain the broad support of workers, peasants, soldiers and businessmen. How can you do this? First, do not emphasize the treatment of intellectuals and the budget for higher education, and do not demand impractical democratic change; for this will alienate the workers and farmers.

The propaganda aimed at the workers, farmers and soldiers must emphasise the fact that the words "owned by the people" actually mean "owned by a small group of bourgeoisie." That group calls us the "masters of the country," yet we live in overcrowded conditions from generation to generation. On the other hand, those "civil servants" build villas, and have police escorts for their luxury cars — while we "masters" travel on crowded buses. Hoisting the flag of stability and unity, they accuse us; when they are the real cause of instability. Can we turn a blind eye to their draining of the national treasury? For where does that money come from? From our sweat and blood. They don't care about the welfare of the nation, in their luxury cars, or playing golf. What is their salary, and how much do they spend? The national output is the income of this small group, who are no different than feudal rulers.

We cannot depend on enlightened rulers, but only on a perfectly democratic system, a free press, an independent judiciary, and people's representatives who are really chosen by the people.

A small group makes use of the press, cheating and tricking the people. The scandal of their existence cannot be exposed, and the people's views cannot be expressed.

The people's representatives are appointed by this bureaucratic bourgeoisie, so how can they represent the people and reflect their concerns?

Dear students, remember the Student Movement of two years ago, when a small group made use of the press to lie to the people, and sow dissension between students on the one hand, and workers and peasants on the other. They said, "To train a university student means spending 10,000 yuan, which is earned by hundreds of workers and peasants; but the students have no respect for that." The real truth is that property is built on the blood and sweat of millions of our comrades, and spent by the small group, who are the biggest of capitalists, and disastrous for the people.

The interests of the workers, peasants and students are the same, and you can have their support.

April 28, 1989

XXXVI: An Open Letter to the Students [23]

Your honorable actions have raised the sympathy of our workers and of the whole society. Speaking from the heart, your worries and concern for China are the same as our own. The rise and fall of a nation is the responsibility of each individual within it.

For various reasons we, the workers, cannot act like the students, coming out on the streets in demonstrations, carrying out a general strike. However, our hearts are as one. We firmly support the seven reasonable requests which you have made. If this is a fight for truth, then death holds nothing to fear.

Although we cannot join your march, we can support you both spiritually and materially; so you do not have to fight alone. If you need money, we can raise it. If you need equipment, we can provide it. The working class will give you its generous support for your self-sacrificing action in the cause of the nation.

I also offer the following advice:

1) Because the official news agency has distorted the facts to keep people ignorant, I suggest that you promote widespread publicity, printing pamphlets, organising information groups, and ensuring that everyone hears the truth.

2) Following the strike, other activities must be promoted, including marches, demonstrations, and petitions, all of which create pressure.

3) Allow more institutions of higher education to join your processions, invite celebrities and important people to make speeches in support, so as to broaden your influence.

4) Hold on to the end in a spirit of self-sacrifice.

Finally, let me thank you again for your righteous action. The future is bright, but the road is winding. The first streak of light is breaking through. Struggle, now, comrades! Let us shout: "Long live democracy, equality and freedom."

[undated]

XXXVII: *Letter to the Workers of the Capital* [24]

Honorable Comrades,

Democracy and dictatorship are in a life or death struggle. The Li Peng government has become isolated and counter-revolutionary, publicly raising the banner of opposition to both democracy and the people. As it moves large numbers of troops towards the city, we see that this wonderful Democracy Movement is going to be swept away. This morning, 3,000 university students went on a hunger strike, but most of the students face a brutal repression. Only the capital's working class can save the Democracy Movement by taking immediate action:

1) Make use of all non-violent means to prevent the troops entering the city, inform the troops about the real nature of the Patriotic-Democratic Movement, its great historical significance, and persuade the troops to support the people.

2) Organise a workers' picket group, maintain order in the capital, prevent illegal behaviour, such as arson, theft and destructive violence, and thereby ensure that the struggle of the student hunger strikers can proceed.

May 13, 1989

XXXVIII: *Declaration of the Preparatory Committee of The Beijing Workers' Autonomous Federation (BWAF)*

It is our understanding that the students' democratic and patriotic Movement, which began in April, has become a national movement which directly influences the interests of the workers.

We understand that, in the national interest, the students have given their all, and that the lives of the hunger strikers are now in danger.

In the interest of those thousands of students, of workers, and of the welfare of the entire nation, we formally declare that the Politburo must unconditionally accept the two student demands within twenty-four hours. Otherwise, beginning on May 20th at noon, there will be a one day general strike, after which we will decide on further steps.

Further, let the workers of the whole nation know that the workers of Beijing are now organised.

May 19, 1989

XXXIX: Public Notice "Number One" of the BWAF

The BWAF is a spontaneous and temporary organization formed by the workers of Beijing in response to the unusual current situation. Its objectives are to fight for democracy, bring down dictatorship, support and protect the student hunger strikers, promote democratization in alliance with the students and citizens from all walks of life. We call for:

1) A general strike in Beijing (with the exception of electricity, water, gas, mail and communications), beginning at noon on May 20th, and lasting until the military withdraw from the city.

2) Opposition to the entry of troops into the city, defence of the Democracy Movement, the maintenance of discipline in Tiananmen Square, the blockage of all main roads into the city and subway exits with vehicles, the maintenance of the normal operation of radio and television broadcasting.

3) The cooperation of all citizens in informing the troops in Beijing concerning the true situation.

May 20, 1989

XL: Public Notice "Number Two" of the BWAF

This afternoon, the Standing Committee of the BWAF called an emergency meeting on our special role in the present situation. As the leading group they a set up secretariat, a public relations section, and a liaison and support section.

1) The BWAF is a Beijing workers' autonomous organization with the objective, democratically and legally, of promoting a Patriotic-Democratic Movement. It invites all workers in the capital to participate actively in our union.

2) Given the present situation, the meeting decided specifically, i) that the present task of the workers' picket group is to maintain a close cooperation with the Students' Autonomous Union, and to guarantee the safety of the students and the stability of Beijing society; and, ii) that the workers' picket group also ensure the movement of the city's resources and daily needs of the citizens, such as transportation and food.

May 21, 1989

XLI: *Declaration of the BWAF Preparatory Committee on Behalf of the Workers*

The working class is the most advanced class and we, in the Democratic Movement, should be prepared to demonstrate its great power.

The People's Republic of China is supposedly led by the working class, and we have every right to drive out the dictators.

The workers know best how to use knowledge and technology in the production process, so we will not permit the destruction of the students, who are of the people.

To bring down dictatorship and totalitarianism and promote democracy in China is our undeniable responsibility.

In the Democracy Movement, "we have nothing to lose but our chains, and a world to win." [25]

May 21, 1989

XLII: *The Initial Programme of BWAF* [26]

Since April 20th the national Patriotic-Democratic Movement, with the students as the vanguard, has enabled the bulk of the working class to demonstrate their desire to discuss and to participate in political matters. At the same time they realised that there was no specifically working class organization to represent them. Under these circumstances, we think that it is necessary to establish an autonomous organization to speak for the workers, to which end we organise BWAF and propose the following initial programme:

1) BWAF allows workers to join on a voluntary basis, is a totally independent organization, has a democratic foundation, and should be regarded as an equal of other people's organizations.

2) The fundamental aim of BWAF is to express the political and economic views of the workers, not just to pursue material ends.

3) BWAF should operate as a supervisor of the activities of the Communist Party.

4) BWAF has the legal right to protect workers in all public organizations and work-places.

5) Under the Constitution BWAF will protect its members from all incursions upon their legal rights.

May 21, 1989.

XLIII: The People in Command [27]

For many years this country, with its population of 1.1 billion, has been under the dictatorship of a handful of bureaucrats who raise the banner of socialism, but who in practice adopt policies that stultify the people and oppress the intellectuals. They are at the peak of the hierarchy, and wield absolute power, beyond any constitutional or party controls. They have an entourage of relatives and associates, and the worst of them is a modern-day Empress Dowager [i.e., Deng Xiaoping]. He manipulates politics from behind a curtain, cares about nothing but his game of bridge, closes his eyes to public suffering, and alienates himself from the masses. The country is trapped in an internal and external debt crisis, and the people's standard of living is reduced by heavy taxes and uncontrollable inflation. It is well known that China is one of the most backward countries in the world, yet he still tries to fool us through manipulation of the media into believing that China has a high GNP.

Does our country still have a place in the international community of nations? Why are we so poor and backward? If the excuse is that our population is too big, how is it that Japan, with its higher population density, fares so well? If the excuse is that other countries have had a longer time to develop, what about Taiwan and South Korea? Why are all these better than us?

In recent years the bureaucrats have become increasingly corrupt, and the leadership more incompetent. Why? People want answers.

Li Peng, you stated that your three children have not been abusing their position for economic advantage. That is not enough, however. As Premier, you must stop all abuses. If, as Premier, you have not been able to root out the most corrupt of the bureaucrats, the most abusive of their power, what are you doing in the job? You people have made a mess of China, a country rich in human and natural resources. It is too easy to say that China lacks experience building socialism, and that you are leading the people across a river, locating each stepping stone as you go. In what direction are you taking us? And what about those who find no stepping stone, and drown? Is the life of the people so worthless that it can be handled like a gambling chip by the bureaucrats?

We have had ten years of reform, and we still don't know where we are going. Who can tell us? Of course you can say, "It doesn't matter what colour the cat, as long as it catches the mouse." But if both cats start fighting over the mouse, only confusion and contradiction follow. Or, put another way, the bureaucratic cat will continue to get fat, and the people will starve. Is that the proper way to run a country?

Premier Zhou Enlai once said, "Who wins the students wins the future." Chairman Mao said, "Whoever represses the student movement will find himself at a dead end." Dust collects if you don't sweep it away. It is the same with reactionaries. We must struggle to bring them down, in the knowledge that, [in Mao's words] political power comes out of the barrel of a gun. We must be prepared to make sacrifices in a fight for democracy. The ruling class will not leave the stage of its own accord, handing democratic rights to us. We must take those rights ourselves. Without democracy, power abuses will remain; and for genuine democracy, the system of permanent officials must be abandoned.

Where there is a one-man dictatorship, democracy is an empty word. Without democracy there are no human rights; and without human rights we are simply slaves. We must not accept this; for we want to be master of the world. Not letting this opportunity slip, we must keep the fire of democracy burning. The evidence shows that the current Democratic Movement is primarily concerned with the question of political power. Only by overthrowing the dictators is there hope for the Movement. In the words of the song of the [wartime] Yenan Anti-Japanese University: "Workers, students, and national bourgeoisie, hasten to the battlefront of our patriotic movement. Listen to the voice of democracy calling. Look, the banner of liberty is flying. We, workers, students, and national bourgeoisie, move together through the torrential storm waves to receive the dawn. Workers, peasants, and national bourgeoisie, rise up, and hasten to the battlefront of our patriotic movement."

Comrades, we oppose some of the party's leaders; but that does not mean that we oppose the party. Also, when we oppose some leaders in the government, we are not rejecting socialism. Is it not the lack of democracy that permits those leaders freely to accuse us of being something which we are not. We must all unite to sweep Deng Xiaoping off the historical stage as soon as possible, save China and her people, and turn over a new page of democracy and freedom.

[Undated]

XLIV: *Aims of the Beijing Construction Workers' Autonomous Union*

This union is formally established on this day, May 21, 1989.
Its aim is as follows:
We are not prison laborers who happen to live in society, but legal citizens of the republic. We want democracy and freedom. The students are demonstrating for the people with their hunger strike. We, Chinese workers, have a conscience, and sympathise with our student brothers and sisters against the wicked government. We must support the students through to the end.

A national crisis lies ahead, and each individual, from both the working class and the professions, must join a union to protect our students. Deng Xiaoping and Li Peng, not knowing how to respond, must be removed by us.

May 21, 1989

XLV: An Open Letter to the Standing Committee of the National People's Congress [28]

This morning we heard that Wan Li, chairman of the Standing Committee, had returned from abroad. We are making an urgent appeal to him.

The third Plenum [of the CCP Central Committee in 1978] forecast a great economic reformation for the whole of China. However, for complex reasons, this developed into a radical economic, political and ideological transformation. We can see that every step in the development of socialism brings forth new ideas and demands for democracy in opposition to the old system and ideas. The Thirteenth Party Congress of the CCP [in 1987] discussed political reform, and adopted a gradualist position. Starting in April, however, the Democratic-Patriotic Movement of university students has generated significant change. Li Peng did not follow the historical trend and opposed the will of the people, arousing their anger and making the situation uncontrollable. Li Peng and his group, not respecting the dignity of the people, have brought shame to the government of the People's Republic of China. The situation could not be worse, and we hope that the Standing Committee will pursue a just solution.

With greatest respect...

May 24, 1989

XLVI: Declaration of the Guandong Workers' Autonomous Union

The GWAU, a local patriotic organization developed within the framework of the nationwide, Patriotic-Democratic Movement, declares itself established. It is an organization initiated by the Guandong workers, and supervised by the citizens, with the purpose of uniting as many elements as possible for the pursuit of freedom, democracy and the well-being of a long-suffering China.

Now that the soldiers have opened fire in Beijing, and the people lie bleeding, the nation has reached a critical juncture. A historical burden falls on the shoulders of every worker. We have no other choice than to oppose the violence, support the students, and promote both democracy and knowledge.

The nation is confused and disrupted, flooded with bureaucracy, with a corrupt political and economic system. The future of the nation has become the personal concern of each individual worker. The Guandong workers cannot stand by, and the GWAU urgently appeals to people from every walk of life to support and participate in the nation-wide, patriotic, Democratic Movement.

June 4, 1989

DISILLUSIONMENT IN THE PARTY

XLVII: Our Suggestions [29]

We are student party members who have taken to the streets to demonstrate with all of the other students, demanding democracy and truth. Each of us has an honest party spirit, and is deeply saddened and disgusted with the corruption, profiteering by officials, and newspaper lies.

We earnestly appeal to the government to open up a dialogue, acknowledge the significance of the Student Movement, and accelerate the process of democratization in China.

We suggest:

1) Do not use freedom of speech for personal attacks, but to discuss constitutional questions.

2) A student strike be staged, without abandoning institutions, to open democratic discussions on the future of China, and of the student autonomous associations.

3) Every party member should think seriously, act honestly, and reject self-seeking behaviour.

April 25, 1989

XLVIII: I Declare my Views [30]

I joined the CCP a few years ago out of unqualified admiration. Its objective is to represent and serve the interests of the people. However, the leaders in this time of conflict are not honest. Therefore, as water can sink the boat which floats upon it, so government can only be popular as it continues to represent the people's interests.

The CCP and our motherland are not identical; and the people love the country before they do the party. The people loved and trusted the party in the 1950's and 1960's. But how much do they trust us today? As a party member I am saddened, for it has lost the trust of the people, which has led to the creation of the Students' Movement. It does not mean that the CCP is no longer great, only that it must represent the interests of the nation if it is to rule legitimately.

Nor are the party central administration and the CCP identical. The people denounce the party centre because it suppresses and lies to the people. This does not mean that the people have ceased to love the party, but that they want immediate reform.

The students' actions are just, and from now on the question of justice follows me everywhere. All conscientious CCP members must open their hearts to the students, and speak the truth. We must defend anyone who represents the interests of the people.

Beijing University, April 30, 1989.

XLIX: The Choice Between Conscience and Party Spirit — An Open Letter to Party Members [31]

Party Comrades,

The hard-line stance of the party is obvious from the analysis of events in the *People's Daily,* and from the general attitudes of party members, which support the position of the central administration.

Deng Xiaoping says, "In Beijing, only 60,000 students have taken part in the strike. One hundred thousand are not involved. We have three million soldiers. What, therefore, do we have to fear?"

The government is probably going to use force to suppress the Democracy Movement; and it seems likely that the march and demonstration planned for tomorrow will develop into another bloody incident.

There are now only two options open to me. I can either be a conscientious Chinese, and conscientious party member, and struggle for democracy and prosperity in China; or I can be a compromised party member, safely maintaining my party membership by uncritical compliance with the demands of the party centre. How should I choose?

Comrade Zhou Enlai once said, speaking to foreign guest, "I am Chinese before I am a party member." Some people would shed blood for democracy and freedom, for the sake of reform. How trivial is party membership and personal interest from this perspective. In fact, the decision of the party centre does not represent the wishes of the party, and we must say this!

Look at the scene. In front of the Great Hall of the People three students hand in a petition, and are ignored. Where is the party spirit of our leaders? Is the party the voice of the people? Who is destroying the party?

The government would use three million soldiers, who are supposed to protect the people, against the Student Movement for freedom and democracy. Is this not dictatorship?

As party members we are not prepared to shed more tears over a corrupt regime and popular indifference. I simply want to be a good communist, working for democracy and freedom, even shedding my blood.

History will prove that those who fight for democracy are the true communists, fighting for the well-being of the nation.

May 3, 1989

L: Support the Actions of the Students! [32]

Today we hear much about the university students in the capital, about their persistent and just actions in the promotion of democracy. This meets with our approval, and we have the deepest respect for their actions.

We hope that those same students understand that all who have reason and a sense of justice, all political and judicial cadres concerned with the strengthening of our nation, will not submit blindly to those pig-headed leaders who oppose the students. We understand and sympathise with the students.

Our position is difficult, and we cannot take up the same stance as you, the students, in the great Democracy Movement. However, we would never go against the tide of history, nor passively watch it. We have faithfully transmitted the platforms, slogans and actions of the students to our colleagues, and have supported the students in various ways.

The students should be satisfied with our position, and history will bear witness that China's elites were not afraid to make sacrifices for the creation of a democratic, prosperous and civilised country.

May 3, 1989

LI: *Quit the Young Communist League!*

In view of the corruption within the Communist Party, and the total despair that it has bred within the people by its responses to the Student Movement, we, members of the Beijing University Young Communist League, as rational and conscientious persons, have lost hope, and show our disillusionment by quitting the League, declaring our full support for the hunger strikers, and opposing the inhuman attitude of our unresponsive government.

May 15, 1989

LII: *Communist Party Members, Step Forward!* [33]

The Patriotic-Democratic Movement has reached a crucial stage, with the hunger strike by thousands of students in Tiananmen Square having entered its seventh day. Yet our leaders have still said nothing in response to their reasonable demands. As members of the CCP we feel that the government's response has been wrong and unwise. Since April 15th we have identified with the Democracy Movement, are disgusted with the erroneous assessment of the government's leaders, and the poor image of the party thus generated.

We treasure our title, members of the Chinese Communist Party. We joined the party to promote communism and, although we have only been in the party for a few years, we value our identity with it. The party member is in the vanguard of revolution, serving the people by example. Our predecessors gave their blood and their lives to give honour to the party, whose name is today tarnished by the current demands for democracy and a rule of law. Since April 20th we have been under considerable pressure not to associate with the Movement as party members, but only as individuals, leading us to reflect deeply upon our commitment and duties as party members. We are not ashamed to stand before the students bearing the proud title of membership, for it is truth that genuine party members defend, not the reputations of particular leaders. Considering specific leaders, we say that they are not true party members. The image of the CCP is not their monopoly, but of all of us.

We assert,
1) that all CCP members should step forward and defend the right of its members to participate in the Patriotic-Democratic Movement *as party members*, which is also in the greatest interest of the people;
2) that the Movement is threatened, and party members should come forward to assist in the organization of autonomous student associations, self-consciously avoiding unnecessary losses in their numbers.

[undated]

LIII: *Urging Deng Xiaoping to Admit His Mistakes — an Open Letter to the CCP* [34]

To the Central Committee and all comrades in the party:
The students are in danger! The situation is perilous! The future of our country is at stake!

Yet the Politburo and State Council continue to ignore the reasonable demands of the student hunger strikers. The conflict is intensifying and the consequences will be dreadful.

As party members, we are immensely concerned. Therefore, we appeal to Comrade Deng Xiaoping to admit openly his mistakes, and acknowledge that his calling the Student Movement a "riot" was entirely wrong. Deng, who is head of neither the party nor of the Standing Committee of the Politburo, is not in possession of decision-making powers. That he should give orders to the whole party is a violation of the party's principles of organization. This kind of imperious behaviour makes a mockery of any claim that there is democracy in the party. We hope that Comrade Deng will value his past achievements, and consider his mistakes from the perspective of the national welfare, so as to solve this problem in perfect honesty.

We want the Politburo to show its party spirit, conscience and courage, follow the wishes of the people and the party, make truly collective decisions, immediately and unequivocally acknowledge this Patriotic-Democratic Movement, consider and comply with the legitimate demands of the students (which are simultaneously the demands of the people), and immediately set out to promote the democracy and the rule of law in our mother country.

History will not give us many chances. The Central Committee and the entire party should act immediately, and make the correct choice for the welfare of our race.

Save the students! Save the nation!

May 18, 1989

LIV: Letter to the People [35]

Dear Students, Citizens of the Republic, Compatriots, Communist Party Members, Soldiers of the PLA,

We must inform you, with great anger and deep sadness, that Zhao Ziyang has certainly resigned from his post as party leader, and that Li Peng has taken charge of the Politburo and ordered an immediate crackdown.

On May 13th Zhao Ziyang proposed to the Standing Committee of the Politburo a renunciation of the April 26th editorial of the *People's Daily*. The proposal was defeated. On May 15 Zhao intended to make a public statement of his views on the matter in Tiananmen Square. The central office of the CCP regarded this as a violation of party rules. Then, on May 16th Zhao presented the following six proposals to the Politburo Standing Committee which was attended by Deng Xiaoping [although he is not now a member]:

1) Repudiate the April 26th editorial.
2) Deng should accept responsibility for the editorial.
3) A special department of the People's Congress should be set up to investigate bureaucratic profiteering by the children of top cadres, including the son of Deng.
4) Provide a full biography of all top cadres.
5) Reveal the salaries and fringe benefits of all top cadres.
6) Cancel the privileges of top cadres.

The Politburo rejected these proposals, and on May 17th a decision to oust Zhao was passed with a narrow majority. Li Peng took over the leadership of the Politburo. Martial law becomes the order of the day, and the repression of May, 1976, is to be repeated.

Yet we live in a different age, and the past will not be repeated. We hear that Wan Li stands with Zhao and will call a meeting of the leaders of the National People's Congress. Li Peng threatens Wan Li with party discipline. And we hear that students are about to go on a new hunger strike. Given all of this, we appeal to all people,

1) to avoid bloodshed and refrain from violence;
2) to initiate a nationwide general strike; and
3) to remind the PLA that it is the child of the people, and should not kill them.

We demand, therefore,

1) a meeting of the Standing Committee of the National People's Congress to dismiss Li Peng from the Premier's position, and
2) a meeting of the Central Committee of the CCP to elect a new General Secretary, and to put an end to the interference of old men behind the scenes.

Dear Students, Citizens, and Compatriots, the Chinese nation is again at a dangerous juncture, with the republic and CCP facing a life and death situation. Let us immediately move to resolve the problem in a non-violent manner.

May 19, 1989

LV: *Statement on Quitting the Party* [36]

Firmly and unequivocally I withdraw from the Communist Party, which has been raped and dishonoured by Deng Xiaoping and Li Peng. This party has destroyed in me the hope and confidence with which I originally associated it. It now stands for opposition to the people. If Deng is the party, and Li represents the party, then I want no truck with it.

Such is my solemn declaration.

May 20, 1989

LVI: *Quit the CCP and Establish a Society for the Promotion of the Chinese Democracy Movement* [37]

To all Patriotic Chinese intellectuals,

The corrupt and incompetent hierarchy of the ruling CCP represses the people, regards democracy as a heresy, ignores the reasonable demands of the patriotic youth, exploits the intellectuals and adopts an attitude of enmity towards them. Therefore, we propose that all intellectuals, who have served the party to this moment, organise themselves into groups and withdraw from the party *en masse*, and establish an organization that can represent the interests of the people. This organization could be called the Society for the Promotion of the Chinese Democratic Movement (Minzhu Hwei — MZH).

The Need to Quit the CCP:

1) The CCP was once a progressive, revolutionary force, but has deteriorated under the conservatism, narrow-mindedness and stupidity of petty peasants.

2) Before it gained power the CCP collaborated with intellectuals, but thereafter, as a tactic in defence of its dictatorship, intellectuals were attacked by the party. The various Anti-Rightist campaigns have been aimed mainly at the intellectuals. Even in better times, intellectuals were used rather than respected by the CCP.

3) The CCP is insincere in its supposed policy of improving teaching conditions and expanding education budgets. Education is of no value to current leaders in their efforts to maintain control.

4) Intellectuals can no longer promote their own or the people's interest through a communist organization. Besides, the reputation of the CCP has been destroyed inside and outside of China. Intellectuals will only taint their own good reputation by being associated with it.

The Procedure for Quitting the Party:

A group of better-known individuals in the field of education and the arts, perhaps a few dozen or a couple of hundreds, must take the lead by publicly quitting the party at a press conference in Beijing. This must be done the day after applying for withdrawal from the party according to its constitution, and the event will be used to publicise the reasons for quitting.

Further, all intellectuals must follow up with a statement of withdrawal. If celebrities cannot be found to initiate the procedure, then the teachers and researchers of Beijing's main institutions of higher education could be coordinated to lead the withdrawal.

Initiation and organization of the MZH:

The CCP cannot represent the interests of the people. The various public organizations are only adjuncts of the party; so we must set up our own organization. In the early stages, mass enrollment at rallies could be used to build up membership. To accommodate intellectuals of various political dispositions the MZH should keep its objectives general — the promotion of political democratization, freedom of the press, independence of the legal system, the punishment of corrupt bureaucrats, and the improvement of education.

Struggle for the Legalization of MZH:

Certainly, the CCP will not agree to the creation of MZH. Thousands of intellectuals will have to join the society to make it an objective reality. This will resemble the Polish Solidarity Movement, which struggled relentlessly until it was recognised. Modern

Chinese history and the Democracy Movement demonstrate that without the organization and support of such a Movement the people and students will lack unity and be suppressed by the government. The most urgent duty of intellectuals at this time is to form a society to counteract the CCP. This is the wish of the people and the hope for democracy. Let us take action now.

[undated]

THE DOUBTS OF SOLDIERS

LVII: From the Bottom of a Soldier's Heart [38]

Dear friends,

You have suffered enough. I speak in the name of all of the generous hearted soldiers of the Third Battalion. The Patriotic Movement of students, workers and citizens has lasted one month. As soldiers, obeying orders, we cannot support you openly. But we are the sons and brothers of the people, Chinese like yourselves, with patriotic hearts. Some young soldiers have created a bad impression in people's minds, but none of us can refuse orders, even the one to advance on the capital. But we say to you: Comrades, don't abandon us, don't treat us badly, for our hearts are linked together, as common people and as Chinese.

You are struggling for democracy and freedom; but, friends, do we soldiers have any democracy and freedom? Of course, the army is different. However, even though we don't have the right to go to Beijing and talk to students, a minority have left their posts and gone into the city, in spite of the consequences. Of course, compared with the people, they amount to but a few. But they represent our general concerns for the people and the students.

Friends, don't treat us like dogs, don't hate us. We will improve your view of us by our manner and our actions. We belong to the people. You have suffered greatly, and we will not remain silent. Let this document support you. It is late, but sincere.

We are proud to be associated with such people! Thank you, friends! I salute you with the greatest respect! Take care!

May 20, 1989.

LVIII: *A Statement to All Soldiers in the PLA Who Have Been Ordered to Enter Beijing* [39]

I am a university teacher who is also the wife of a soldier, and the daughter of a soldier. At this moment our students are in Tiananmen Square opposing the mad ideas of Li Peng. It is reported that you are on the outskirts of Beijing. Therefore, you have probably heard of the million-strong support of the students' Patriotic-Democracy Movement. Li Peng's government having misled you, the people must tell you the truth. The people everywhere, with the students, are in a struggle with Li Peng's government, which has in its statements and actions shown itself to be useless.

I think that truth will defeat the evil. Because you were uninformed, I was extremely worried by your arrival. Now I am eager to tell you that, although I regard you with affection, I love these honest and beautiful students more; for they have placed themselves in a life and death situation, and they are supported by the millions of honest citizens of Beijing. I beg you not to fight, not to brutalise the citizens and students of our capital; for in so doing you will be changed from our saviors into the most hated persons in all history.

With tears in my eyes, as a member of your family, I beg you not to touch our students, or arouse the people's anger. Li Peng is in the wrong, but the people will forgive you. If you attack, however, you will be criminals forever.

With my son in my arms, I will stand before you; and if you move forwards, please drive over our bodies.

May 21, 1989

LIX: A Letter to all Soldiers [40]

To all soldiers in the army:

You have often said that your guns will not be used against the people. I believe this absolutely. But think about this. After you have entered Beijing, will the government stop oppressing the people as you think? Just look at what Li Peng has said recently. First he has said that the students are patriotic, then that they are causing turmoil. Given such contradictory statements, who can trust him? In all seriousness, the government is using you to suppress the people. You must not enter Beijing; for this would make you criminals of historical dimensions.

May 22, 1989

LX: An Open Letter to the Students [41]

A salute to you from an old soldier! Over the past few days I have been watching your struggle, and want to remind you that you have already achieved an incredible victory. I cannot openly support you, but I can advise you of the following.

1) *On questions of strategy:* If there are several hundred thousand people in Tiananmen Square, the much smaller number of soldiers will not be able to handle the situation. Even though we have had martial law for a few days, no military action has taken place in the square, for there are not enough soldiers and policemen. Further, because of their training, they will find it difficult to shoot the people. The ten million people of Beijing, united together, are unconquerable.

2) *On questions of tactics:*

   i) *Road junctions:* That people have blocked military vehicles is unprecedented. Never retreat. Even if a few platoons get through, they will be insufficient. Therefore, improve your command system and organization here, as it is sometimes poor.

   ii) *Splitting:* A familiar tactic to be used against the army. Permit say two-thirds of the soldiers to pass, and then block the remainder. Repeat this at each junction, thus cutting the army into several separate parts which cannot cooperate. In this way, the power and the initiative of the army will evaporate.

iii) *Shooting and tear gas:* In a crowd of several thousands, this can cause confusion, injuries and deaths. We must warn the army commanders who give such orders that they will be sentenced to death by courts martial. And even if Beijing can be controlled by means of a massacre, can the whole of China? We don't have enough armies.

iv) We should trust the basic qualities of the People's Army, the product of deep and detailed ideological work. Ask them not only to refrain from entering the city, but also to stand alongside the people.

Hoping for victory for the people of Beijing!

May 22, 1989

LXI: A Letter to all Soldiers who are Ordered to Enter Beijing to Impose Martial Law [42]

Dear Warriors,

I am also a soldier, born in a peasant family. We are brothers, from the same class, fellow soldiers in the same trench. As your senior, I want to discuss with you your responsibility as soldiers.

The PLA is the army of the people, the sons and brothers of workers and peasants, standing close to them, service to them being our main purpose, and through which we show that we are not a private army of a warlord.

If foreigners invade our country, then we will sacrifice ourselves willingly on the battlefields. In times of natural disaster, we immediately go to the aid of affected areas, risking our lives. In the hearts of our people the PLA are secure, like fish in water.

It is sad for me to tell you that you are not here to fight enemies of the people, nor to combat a disaster. You have been deceived; for the army comes to Beijing to suppress the patriotic Student Movement; and when you fight your way into Beijing, you will be starting a civil war.

The movement which has been initiated by the students, and supported by the workers, peasants, and intellectuals, affects everyone. Its goals are the promotion of reform, to attack corruption, ending bureaucratic speculation on the black market, and the improvement of the standard of living of the entire population. In an event unprecedented in world history, one million people participated in a demonstration in Beijing. This is a Movement of the same historical importance as with the May Fourth Movement of 1919. It attacks the privileged and corrupt elements, like Yang Shangkun. Yang, purged by Mao Zedong, was saved by the party, and given important powers. However, after he became Vice-Chairman of the Military Commission, he used his authority to appoint his brother, Yang Baibang, to head of the Political Department, and his son to the leadership of the 2nd Armed Battalion. To his shame, the meeting of the Military Commission has become a family affair!

The core of the CCP must agree with the patriotic views of the students, and reject the view that the Movement has created "turmoil." That would mean that it is counter-revolutionary, which is ridiculous. The core of the party supports the students' criticism of bureaucratic corruption; and the Yang brothers fear for their feudal privileges. Regardless of popular discontent, Yang and his clique openly expel Zhao Ziyang, General Secretary of the CCP. They support the ambitions of Li Peng, who has just committed the error of declaring martial law, and have usurped the power of the party by ordering 100,000 troops to surround Beijing. Their main aim is to suppress the students' Patriotic-Democracy Movement, and to organise a cover-up. Their second purpose is to foment disorder so as to establish a fascist dictatorship, a Yang dynasty. They are outrageous, obvious, and opposed by senior commanders of the PLA. Some even mouth the slogan, "Down with the new warlord!"

Given this, why do large numbers of armed soldiers, with their tanks and their guns, enter the peaceful capital? Was there a military rebellion? No! Rioting, arson, and illegality? No! There is merely a peaceful demonstration by unarmed students, a student strike, a rally, a sit-down hunger strike. If we are supposed to be tackling a small minority of bad people, why do we need 100,000 soldiers?

Brothers, you see the attitudes of the common people, as they block our convoys with their bodies, trying to save the students and intellectuals. China has reached an important historical movement, and we must be careful to avoid stupid and cruel actions. We must refuse to be servants of the Brothers Yang, refuse to be criminals, refuse to point our weapons at the students and common people. Even if we are punished, we must not be the indifferent tools for a bloody incident. The students will remember us for this, as their parents will support us, and everybody thank us. This is the viewpoint of many soldiers.

I salute you.

May 23, 1989

THE INTELLECTUALS COMMENT

LXII: Declaration of May 17, 1989 (by Yan Jiaqi, Bao Zunxin, Ni Nanyou, Lang Lujun).

Since 2:00 p.m. on May 13th, about three thousand students have been on hunger strike; that is, for more than one hundred hours. More than seven hundred have lost consciousness. This is an unprecedented tragedy in the history of our mother country. The students are asking for a denunciation of the April 26th editorial in the *People's Daily* and the live broadcast of a dialogue between student and government representatives. The children of the mother country are collapsing, and the government is ignoring their demands. So the hunger strike goes on.

Now the problems of our country are exposed to the whole world; and that problem is that an autocrat has unlimited power, with government ignoring its responsibilities and losing all humanity. Such an irresponsible and inhuman government is what we have in our People's Republic: an autocracy.

The Qing dynasty collapsed seventy-eight years ago; yet China still has an emperor, though untitled — a senile autocrat. Yesterday afternoon the General Secretary of the Party, Zhao Ziyang, declared openly that in China all important decisions must be approved by this old man [Deng Xiaoping]. Unless he agrees, the April 26th editorial cannot be denounced. After one hundred hours of starvation, we are left with no other choice than to rely on the people themselves. In this context, we can say that the hunger strike has been a remarkable victory, demonstrating not the "riot" of which the students are accused, but the birth of a Patriotic-Democratic Movement that will bury China's last autocrat and China's last imperial regime.

Let us proclaim:

Victory for the struggle of the hunger strikers! Long live the spirit of non-violent protest!

Down with autocracy! Down with the April 26th editorial! Long live the people! Long live democracy! Long live freedom!

LXIII: An Extremely Urgent Appeal to the People of Beijing [43]

The ruling clique of the military government is blatantly violating the Constitution and openly acting as the enemy of the people. It has proclaimed martial law. The Chinese people are facing a life and death situation. The people, the students and the intelligentsia are facing immediate and bloody persecution. In order to save the republic, we members of the intelligentsia are making these extremely urgent proposals.

1. We urgently call on the 10 million people in the capital to assemble at 1.30 p.m. on May 23rd at Fuxiamen and Jianguomen for a massive procession. The common slogan should be, "Lift Martial Law; Li Peng and Yang Shangkun resign!" We shall have the greatest demonstration for justice in human history, influencing world public opinion in support of our own one billion people.

2. We must strengthen and continue our propaganda work with the People's Liberation Army. Our slogan should be, "Do not stain your hands with the blood of the people." We will wage a massive all-out campaign that includes members of high schools, primary schools, and kindergartens. Our aim is to demoralise the military and convince it to take the side of the people.

3. Immediately convene an extraordinary meeting of the people's congress of the Beijing municipality; sack [Mayor] Chen Xitong;

annul all curfew orders; and elect a new government; restore the public transportation system, law and order, and create a new social order for the people.

4. Urge all the politicians and military personnel who have a conscience to make clear their position and to use their influence in the military regions to support the people of the capital, and to send immediate help to save the people's republic.

5. We must have no illusions about the ruling clique of the militarist government. We must be clearly aware of the imminence of a large-scale and bloody conflict. All the citizens should organise themselves immediately and should establish a unified network for co-ordination, directives and mobilization. We must prevent the military from being able to crush us with a few concentrated attacks. We must also be prepared to sacrifice blood, and so must organise first aid and medical facilities.

6. If the militarist government is prepared to risk the condemnation of the whole world by resorting to bloody terror to suppress the masses, and install an autocratic rule, the people in the capital must disperse immediately and try to protect the student leaders and the vanguard among the intelligentsia. The people should call for the resolute resistance by the whole nation. The ruling clique will be buried by the resistance of one billion people. When victory is gained, the violators of the Constitution will be brought to justice for their crimes, and a new era for the republic will begin.

Dear people of the capital. This is the last fight and the last hope of the republic. With all your passion and courage, defend the People's Republic with your blood and your lives.

May 22, 1989

LXIV: To All Compatriots [44]

Since April 15th, a Patriotic-Democratic Movement, instigated by the Beijing students, has swept through China, creating a following inside and outside the country. However, the development of the movement is seriously threatened by a handful of reactionaries, like Li Peng. Fellow countrymen, note that the outcome of this movement will affect us all.

The movement's aim is to combat corruption and autocracy, and to fight for democracy. However, China has entrenched problems of a centralised autocracy and a self-protective ruling clique. The right of the people to freedom of speech and participation in political life has never been realised. Lies are normal in the media. As for freedom of thought, the media have always been ruthlessly suppressed, and lies are normal in the press. The abuse of power by experts and officials becomes dominant, and the anger of the people against it is expressed in anything that is symbolically useful. At such a moment, the people of Beijing found an outlet in the ceremonies associated with the death of Hu Yaobang:

April 20th: About 100 students were vigorously beaten up by the police for laying a wreath in memory of Yu Haobang [who had died on April 15th] at Zhongnanhai.

April 22nd: Three students, holding more than 100,000 signatures, knelt on the steps before the Great Hall of the People in Tiananmen Square, requesting that Li Peng accept the petition. They were ignored, even though Li Peng and other party and government leaders were in the hall.

April 24th: The chief editor of the *World Economic Herald* was sacked, and control of the press intensified.

April 25th: After listening to a few reports by party leaders, Deng denounced the student movement as a "disturbance," a "turmoil." He also said, "we have an army of three millions," and do not have to fear the curses of anyone in the international community. His words were, "The softer we seem, the more weak we shall become." The next day, an editorial in the *People's Daily*, entitled "Oppose Disturbances Unrelentingly," was obviously based on Deng's speech. It asserted that the student movement was an anti-party and anti-socialist disturbance.

April 27th: More than 100,000 students, backed by an enraged public, broke through the blockade of the army and police and staged a demonstration of unprecedented size. Slogans like "Freedom and Democracy" and "Down with Official Corruption" were heard. They also demanded an open, sincere and equal dialogue with the central authorities; which responded by sending in the 38th Army to threaten the students.

April 29th: The authorities held a fake "dialogue" with some officially-appointed student representatives as a mode of deception, whilst continuing to denounce the Student Movement as a "turmoil."

May 4th: A demonstration spread throughout the country, supporting the *World Economic Herald,* demanding freedom and openness[45] in politics. Zhao Ziyang publicised his view that problems had to be solved by democratic means, and within the bounds of the legal system. The students agreed to return to classes, but continued to demand a dialogue.

May 13th: The government had refused to enter into dialogue. Some students were so outraged that they went on a hunger strike. Thus began the conflict that moved the world to tears.

May 18th: On the sixth day of the hunger strike more than 2000 of the hunger strikers had lost consciousness, and many were in danger of contracting sicknesses associated with malnutrition and dehydration. Millions had given their public support. On the same day, Li Peng agreed to meet student representatives, but refused to discuss the circumstances of the hunger strikers. He also said that neither the government nor the party centre had said that the students were creating a disturbance.

May 19th: At 9:00 p.m., following a visit and statement by Zhao Ziyang, the students decided to call off the hunger strike. However, one hour later, Li Peng called a meeting of party cadres at which the student movement was officially called a riot. Worse yet, 100,000 troops were mobilised and, armed to the teeth, at about midnight, began to move on Beijing with tanks, armoured cars, tear gas and high pressure water hoses. The order was not successfully carried out only because the citizens of Beijing spontaneously organised a blockade, and the troops refused to clash with the people.

May 20th: Li Peng declared martial law in Beijing. The city government shut down public transport and ordered the traffic police to quit their posts in order to accuse the students of fomenting public disorder. However, with the active intervention of the students, traffic stayed in good order. No incidents of street fighting or robbery occurred, and social order was maintained.

May 23rd: There has been the most massive popular demonstration against martial law. As for the soldiers, they are insulted by the facile arguments that they have been sent to Beijing "on manoeuvres," or to do "relief work," or, the most stupid, "to make a film." Some high ranking officials have appealed to the Military Committee[46], demanding that the troops refrain from firing on the people, and that martial law be ended. In the afternoon, millions of people, from all walks of life, marched in torrential rain to condemn the handful of persons around Li Peng for antagonising the people, creating social disorder by the cruelest means (whilst blaming the people), and choosing violence as a way of solving the problems arising within our democracy and legal system. Their contemptible goal is to usurp the highest power of the party and the State. The people are demonstrating against this, against their militarism and their willingness to disturb the peace and good order of the capital.

In this Movement, the students have put forward reasonable demands in a legal manner. They have been extremely rational, calm and disciplined, insisting that problems be solved by democratic and legal means. Conditions have degenerated to their present sorry state because of the government's failure to respond. Ignoring the students' physical well-being, distorting public information, and stubbornly upholding its mistakes, the Li Peng government has lost the support of the party and the people. Thoroughly corrupt, it cannot desist, and it will destroy the People's Republic if permitted. Therefore,

1) Determine to carry the Movement through to victory as a precondition of a solution to the present crisis and the future civilised existence of our nation.

2) Demand the earliest end of martial law and the removal of the troops from Beijing; for production, transport, and daily life are operating normally.

3) The People's National Congress or its Standing Committee must immediately convene an emergency meeting to acknowledge the Movement and condemn the April 26th editorial.

4) Li Peng should be taken from office, since he has broken the law in his dealings with the Student Movement; and the government changed.

5) The government must permit freedom of the press, and the people must be permitted to publish their own newspaper. An open political process must ensure that decisions are really made by the people.

6) We must ensure that the government carries through the on-going reforms to their conclusion, the government and people co-operating to overcome difficulties.

Compatriots, the Patriotic-Democratic Movement has been re-vealed. It is a new beginning in China's history, and a major element in the democratic trend that now dominates world history. Before the eyes of the world it has shown itself to reflect the vigour, strength and self-confidence of China and her people. But the democratization process is long, and the people must be determined in their commitment. Only when every Chinese raises his/her fist in righteous support will the last stronghold of the autocratic dynasty crumble into ashes before the roar of the people.

Long live the people! Long live the Republic!

May 24, 1989

A CHINESE SOLIDARITY IN THE MAKING

LXV: Introducing the "Capital Union"

1. The Union of all Sections of the People of Beijing is known by a shortened name "Capital Union."

2. The Capital Union is based on the present, great Patriotic-Demo-cratic Movement. It has been spontaneously organised, and is a mass organization of the masses of workers, intellectuals, cadres of the state machinery, young students, patriotic-democratic elements, peasants and people engaged in business.

3. The goal of the Capital Union is to unite the different sections of people in the capital. We call on all patriots from different sections,

all parties and factions to take action to set up a patriotic-democratic united front, so that the democratic forces can grow and increase in strength, and the republic be taken along the road of freedom, democracy, the rule of law and civilization.

4. The immediate goal of the Capital Union is to mobilise all patriotic people to actively assist ASUBU and other autonomous organizations in the post secondary field, and to support resolutely the present Patriotic-Democratic Movement to the very end.

5. The immediate tasks of the Capital Union will include:

   a) With the help of the masses of news workers, to publish an unofficial publication that will reflect the true feeling of the people — "the Voice of the People."

   b) The organization of citizen patrol groups to assist the students in maintaining order in the capital, that normal life and social stability will be guaranteed.

   c) The mobilization of the masses from all sections of the community to do everything possible to resist martial law, and thoroughly defeat the conspiracy of military rule imposed by the small clique of autocratic elements.

   d) The study of strategy and tactics for the furthering of the Movement, providing reliable information, practical theories, and suggestions for solving the problems of all patriotic organizations.

   e) The co-ordination of the patriotic elements of all sections of the community so that purposeful, prepared, organised, forceful and united actions can be undertaken against the minority of autocratic forces, and in support of the university students.

   f) The collection of opinions and suggestions from all patriotic elements of the community. Endless efforts will be devoted to promote the maturity and perfection of the Capital Union.

6. The Capital Union will have the following departments: theory and research, strategy and tactics, information, fund-raising, propaganda and agitation, liaison, coordination, supply, editorial board of the "People's Voice," publication, and defense departments.

7. Capital Union bases its action on the will of the majority of China's citizens. The Capital Union supports the Constitution and will work within the Constitution, although it feels that the constitution still needs to be amended and perfected.

8. The precondition for the dissolution of the Capital Union is: — after extensive and sufficient polling of public opinion, it is found that the majority of the Chinese people no longer feel that it should continue to exist. Unless this happens, no other factors or force could bring about its dissolution. The hatred and repression by the autocratic forces will only lead to the growth and the perfection of the Union.

9. The Capital Union is in a condition of continuous development. It is hoped that patriotic elements and organizations of various sectors would give their sincere help and guidance. All help and support, in the form of material or otherwise, are welcome. All sectors of the community are also welcome to join.

Long Live Democracy! Long Live the People!
Long Live Freedom! Long Live China!
Unite and pursue the Democracy Movement to the end!

May 25, 1989

NOTES

1. The *dazibao*, sometimes translated as "big character poster," posted in a public place, is a popular vehicle for the circumvention of censorship controls and providing criticism of the government. They are usually, but not invariably, anonymous. Mao Zedong himself had used it in 1966 to ininitiate the Cultural Revolution. The Xidan Democracy Wall Movement of 1978-1979 was centred on this kind of activity.
2. The distinction here is between a professional party member, who is paid by the CCP to perform a specific task, and regular members whose occupation is with a non-party organization.
3. This pamphlet appeared under the authorship of "A Revolutionary of the Beijing Teachers' Training University."
4. Signed by a "Disciple of Marxism."
5. Anonymous big character poster at the People's University.
6. The pamphlet was prepared by the Theory and Information section of the Beijing University Preparatory Committee.
7. Presented under the authorship, "A Revolutionist of the Teachers' University."
8. Issued by the Autonomous Students' Association of the University of Education of Beijing.
9. Produced by the Xinhua students.
10. Pamphlet distributed at the military camp at Six Mile Bridge, on the western periphery of Beijing.
11. The 38th Army, initially ordered to repress the students and citizens of Beijing, was heroically reticent. Its commander-in-chief, Xu Qinxian, received a prison sentence of 18 years for checking himself into a hospital, preferring to take sick leave to the task of executioner of innocents.
12. This document appeared under the aegis of the Beijing Teachers Training University Students' Autonomous Union on May 28, 1989. It praises the authentic "workers' picket," condemning the government for organising an anti-student segment of workers, with which it should not be confused.
13. Presented by the Autonomous Students' Union of the University of Science and Technology, under the authority of "Dreaming of China's Emergence."

14. General Secretary of the CCP, removed in 1928.
15. Leader of the Fourth Front army who split with Mao in 1935 during the Long March.
16. Denounced by Mao in 1938 for promoting "formalism of a foreign origin." Wang had just returned from Moscow.
17. Referring to Liu Xiaoqi, Deng Xiaoping, and Zhou Enlai, all of whom were accused of being revisionists of different degrees during the Cultural Revolution.
18. Lin had been designated Mao's heir in 1969, but died two years later in an air crash whilst fleeing to the USSR, supposedly after an attempt to assassinate Mao. Jiang Qing was Mao's wife, member of the infamous Gang of Four, imprisoned in 1981 for heinous crimes committed during the Cultural Revolution.
19. The next three documents appeared under the authority of the "Beijing Workers' Union."
20. The CCP distrust of intellectuals was seen during the Cultural Revolution when they were called the "stinking ninth" after the other specified "class enemies,": i) landlords, ii) rich peasants, iii) counter-revolutionaries, iv) "bad elements," v) rightists, vi) renegades, vii) enemy agents, and viii) capitalist-roaders.
21. At the time of writing, Deng Xiaoping was perhaps the most powerful man in China, although his formal position was simply Chairman of the Military Commission of the CCP. Zhao Ziyang was General Secretary of the CCP (soon to be removed for being opposed to the use of military force against the demonstrators) and Li Peng was Premier of China. In an intra-party conflict between Zhao and Li, the latter was able to swing the reactionary forces behind him. Those reactionaries are typified by the other names here: Yang Shangkun (President of China), Chen Yun (85-year old chairman of the CCP Central Advisory Commission), Li Xiannian (80-year old former President), Peng Zhen (87-year old former Premier), and Jiang Zemin (62) who was to replace Zhao Ziyang as General Secretary of the CCP.
22. Signed by "A Worker."
23. Signed by "A Beijing Worker."

24. The document appears under the sponsorship of The Chinese Workers' Movement College Committee in Support of Student Action, Capital Workers' Picket Group Temporary Command Centre.
25. An obvious reference to the final lines of *The Manifesto of the Communist Party* (1848), written by Marx and Engels.
26. As presented by the Preparatory Committee of BWAF.
27. Release by BWAF.
28. Presented by "Workers' representatives."
29. By "A Group of Marxists."
30. By "a party member."
31. By a "Beijing University student CCP member."
32. By "Cadres of the Security and Judiciary Departments."
33. By student members of the CCP.
34. This piece originated in Beijing University under the authorship of "Members of the CCP."
35. By "Some Cadres of Central State Institutions."
36. By Zhu X..., "Teacher of English."
37. By "Some Teachers and Party Members of the People's University."
38. By "A Soldier of the Third Battalion of the Central Security Guards."
39. By "A Soldier's Wife."
40. By "A Member of the PLA," handed out at Beijing University.
41. By "An Old Soldier."
42. By an "Army Colonel."
43. Presented by "Intellectuals in the Capital."
44. Presented by "Intellectuals of the Capital."
45. *Glasnost,* or openness, was the official policy in the USSR, which was moving rapidly towards a position of *rapprochement* with the PRC. The Chinese students quite obviously viewed the Soviet developments as an encouraging sign. However, when Mikhail Gorbachev visited China in May, 1989, he deliberately distanced himself from the Movement, refusing comment.
46. This could refer to the Military Committee of the National People's Congress (a government body), or to the Military Commission of the CCP, the chairman of which was Deng Xiaoping at that time.

III

INTERVIEWS WITH THREE
LEADING PERSONALITIES

LXVI: Two Interviews With Wuer Kaixi [1]

[Interviewer's Introduction]

Commenting on his relationship with Wang Dan, Wuer Kaixi stated that he was both a friend and comrade in arms, although it was possible that they could become political opponents. By contrast with Wang's quiet determination, Wuer presents himself energetically and forcefully, with confidence and bluntness. By contrast, Wang stands quietly to one side, lets Wuer hold forth, occasionally reminding him of a point or adding a qualification. They never quarrel or compete for power.

On May 8, 1989, Wuer had led his classmates from the Beijing University of Education to Tiananmen Square to support a demonstration being held by the Association of Chinese Reporters. He looked for Wang around the square, shouting his name, and was disappointed not to find him. After the May Fourth Demonstration Wang had said that he was going to quit the Student Movement.

Tired and depressed, he said that he would rather work on creating a Democratic Movement. However, when the hunger strike got under way the two began again to cooperate.

At 3:00 a.m. on May 21st Wuer was under tremendous pressure to quit Tiananmen Square, and did so. The rumour was that a representative of the Foundation of the Disabled (which is headed by the son of Deng Xiaoping, Deng Paofang) told him that the army was going to march into the square and kill all of the students. Wuer was not widely condemned for his action, although some students stopped supporting him. Moreover, some of the Beijing students disliked his "individualism," his love of fun, his tendency to make independent decisions, and the fact that he always had a girl in tow.

Only twenty years old, Wuer Kaixi is an ethnic Turk from Sinkiang province. His father has a modest position on a newspaper there, so it is wrong to call the young man the son of a high official. Any money he spends is earned from providing economic articles for the Sinkiang press. The greatest influence on him is his teacher in the Faculty of Chinese at the Beijing Normal University, the Doctor of Literature, Liu Xiaobo, whom Wuer admits to consulting. [2]

After the April 27th demonstration the Student Movement became quiet for some days. Student leaders, including Wuer and Wang, sought to generate an atmosphere of interest and activism for a demonstration on May 4th. Wuer went into hiding, some students claimed that their lives were in danger, and others said that they were about to be arrested by the police. Later on, after the demonstration, they admitted that this had been a strategy to ensure that the students' spirits could be easily aroused.

In Tiananmen Square both young and old approach Wuer for his autograph, even visitors from Hong Kong. Nor is it just ordinary people who admire him; for even experienced reporters ask their colleagues to get his autograph, with some words of greeting. Wuer is quite the star, and apparently enjoys it. He also has the attributes of a celebrity, with a ready smile, clever speech, delighting in the self-conscious use of his talents. He also recognises his own weaknesses, and people seem willing to accept the sincere apologies that follow his mistakes.

These interviews were conducted on June 2nd and June 3rd. It was still a peaceful situation, and his manner was relaxed. Nevertheless, his confidence, courage and faith in democracy are all evident.

The First Interview

Question: After the successful demonstrations of April 27th and May 4th, why did students take part in a hunger strike?

Answer: After demonstrations, marches, and sit-ins, this peaceful action became most significant. The idea was proposed by Wang Meng, Wang Dan, Chin Chiang, Yang Chaofai, Ma Siufang and myself. The hunger strikers demanded democracy, and were prepared to sacrifice their lives for that end. The University of Beijing and the Beijing University of Education were its organizers.

Q: How did you feel when you saw those students being carried unconscious from the square?

A: As an organiser I was, of course, anxious and sad; but their commitment had to be respected.

Q: The hunger strike lasted for seven days, and did not achieve its objectives. Was it foolish? Why was it stopped?

A: We estimated that the government would enter into a dialogue with us before the hunger strike was three days old; but it was too stupid and shameless. The students entered voluntarily into the action, and were prepared to die even if nothing were achieved.

It is not foolish to die for the future greatness of China. It is something that is to be respected. We stopped the strike once we recognised that the government was stupid and blind to that. It would have been childish and silly to use the bodies of decent students to seek change from such a government. During the strike we matured, and came to see that we must have a revolution. Our definitive slogan became, "Li Peng! Step Down!"

Q: Some intellectuals had told you to stop the strike for the sake of the students' health. Why did you ignore them?

A: They could have persuaded us if they had treated us correctly. However, they adopted an authoritarian posture, and in condescending to us aroused discontent. They should have treated us like equals. We are all citizens; and students are not simpletons.

Q: The Student Movement has been turned into a weapon employed in the power struggle amongst the top government leaders.

A: That's none of our business. We have our own agenda; and I have no faith in the view that the Student Movement can win by means of the help of a particular group of government officials. The Student Movement will have achieved its grand purpose when the Chinese people demand the resignation of the government, voicing their great dissatisfaction with the leaders of this country. This transformation of consciousness is the first step, which must then produce a democratic society. This weapon, the Student Movement, too big for the bureaucrats to cope with, directly promotes the struggle of democracy against the power of conservatism.

Q: If you had retreated after two or three days of your hunger strike, when Li Peng met the students' representatives, would you have achieved a better result?

A: If China is to move forward she must get more than "wise leaders." Political power must be controlled, and a democratic system introduced. If we had stopped the strike to talk with Li Peng, and the government had accepted our demands, such as admitting corruption, we might have shouted, "Long live Li Peng!" But this would never have led to our current demands of "freedom of the press" and "self-governing organizations."

Let me emphasise that whether Li Peng steps down or not is unimportant compared with the broad acceptance of our slogans, which will mean social pressure to place constraints upon government. If Li Peng were to step down, to be replaced by some other party figure, it would mean nothing. Even if Zhao Ziyang retains power, and is a good secretary, restraints should also be placed on him. We will have shouted the slogan, but seen no substantial change. The Democracy Movement wants to achieve: 1) democratic consciousness, and 2) a democratic institutional structure. That is the foundation upon which we must build. It will be a long and hard process, and I am prepared to devote the rest of my life to the task.

Q: But now we see a reactionary government imposing harsher controls.

A: I believe that this restrictive policy will be temporary, and that it contains a time bomb. It will generate a huge opposition. Democracy will not be achieved overnight, but our efforts can hasten its coming. I predict that there will be changes in the next three to five years.

Q: Earlier, when the students held a dialogue with Li Peng, why did you interrupt his speech?

A: We were sitting in the air-conditioned Hall of the People, on a sofa drinking tea. Outside there were hungry students sitting on the cold ground of Tiananmen Square. Li Peng began to deliver a long opening speech, treating the students like immature children. He spoke nonsense, presented no solutions, and did not respect the people's rights. He should rather treat himself as a child of the people, a civil servant of the people and the country; but he was just too proud. We were told that his son's involvement, or non-involvement, in corrupt practices was none of our business. It was all a waste of time. His behaviour as the Premier made us sick. After three minutes we had had enough, and I just had to stop him.

Q: Everyone thinks that you had a lot of guts to interrupt his speech on television. Were you treating him like a Premier?

A: [Angrily] I treated him like a citizen. To be a Premier is his work. As a citizen of the republic I am his equal. I am more honest than he; and if we are unequal, then it is I who must be his superior, not the reverse. But I think that we are equal; so I did not need to be afraid when I interrupted his speech.

Q: Some have said that you pretended to faint at that time.

A: No. I had an asthma attack because I was so angry. I lost all my strength and had to lie down for an oxygen tube to be inserted in my nose. By then the dialogue had failed with Li Peng's bad performance. Wang Dan told me to leave, and I replied, "Please carry me away."

Q: Did your questioning of Li Peng during the national broadcast have any consequences?

A: Tremendous consequences. We met as two citizens, which is natural. However, in the words of the Hou Dejian's song, "We are not used to it." In the past, to meet the Premier was a "generous gift" from the government. My performance was a beginning. People are tired of that kind of feudalism, and are delighted to see equality.

Q: Do you think that your popularity is widespread?

A: Yes, especially in Beijing. I am, however, sad when someone shouts, "Long live Wuer Kaixi." I work for the Democracy Movement, and am opposed to dictatorship and the feudal empire. Someone wanted *me* to be long-lived; but other people have suffered a great deal more.

Q: People look upon you as the student star.

A: I am willing to be a hero, which is natural, even though I'm not worthy of it. As for being a "star", what can I do about it [with a big grin]?

Q: You are criticised for being too individualistic.

A: That's the fault of the reporters, who build up an imaginary picture by emphasising my positive aspects. I have always said that I have many weaknesses. One can only aspire to perfection.

Q: People say that you overly enjoy attractive clothes, spending money, and having a good time.

A: [Angrily again]. That's stupid. I'm an ordinary person, so why can't I enjoy good clothes, good food and good company? Why must I be solemn, and look as bad as Li Peng?

Q: There are rumours that foreign countries would provide political protection for student leaders.

A: There are many such rumours, but I don't pay any attention to them. We must struggle and sacrifice, not escape, which is useless for the Democratic Movement. It is better to be in jail. But I'm willing to travel, have a look at the U.S.A., Hong Kong, Taiwan, and Macau. I want study and experience; but I never want to lose touch with China. I am closely linked with the Democratic Movement, and would devote my life to it. I think about my personal contribution, and carry out my historical responsibility as an active person who loves literature, art and life. That is my conclusion. If Wang Dan or I were to quit it would be truly irresponsible in relation to the Movement, as much as I love life.

Q: You mean, "enjoy life?"

A: [Smile]

Q: Let's talk about the interesting matter of your relationship with Wang Dan.

A: Of course. We have been friends and comrades since the beginning of the Student Movement. He is a person whose behaviour and conduct are ever exemplary. Although we don't always agree, we cooperate always for the sake of the Movement. He was not happy for a period of time, and moved from the Square to Beijing

University. However, even if we were to become political opponents, we would always be friends.

Q: Before the 1989 Student Movement, nobody knew who you were. By contrast, Wang was promoting democracy earlier with such organizations as the "Democracy Field Salon."

A: I'm not sensitive about this. As a first year student at the Beijing University of Education I have only been in university for seven or eight months.

Q: You are always optimistic — unlike Wang, who is sometimes pessimistic. Is there anything in your family background that explains this? Do your parents support you?

A: My parents have encouraged me. My mother visited me on May 17th when I had just started the hunger strike. They were concerned about my poor health; for I have a heart infection and low blood sugar. I have been in hospital on ten occasions, and lose consciousness when I get over-excited. Although I was born in Beijing, my family moved to Sinkiang in 1984. I returned in 1987 to complete my high school studies. I had also been involved in the students' union of my secondary school in Sinkiang.

Q: You have reiterated the criticism of intellectuals as "the stinking ninth." [3] Why are you unhappy with them? Would you regret the loss of their support?

A: Intellectuals have had a distorted view for thousands of years, favouring reformism rather than revolution.

Q: Does this mean that reform is impossible?

A: Is anything really impossible? People get overly pessimistic. Ten years ago the time was ripe, and still we do so little.

Q: More recently it has been said that the students and their leaders have been demoralised by divisions and sectarianism.

A: The Student Movement is fundamentally magnificent, and beyond criticism. However, since it has a highly complex membership, it is to be expected that there will be traitors within the membership. Its honesty and cohesion can be undermined by,

    i) monetary donations,

    ii) corruptions of power, and

    iii) exaggeration of the ability of student leaders — we all must control ourselves if we are being flattered!

Q: Why don't you all leave the Square? Is it now too late?

A: Actually, we have considered retreat often. On May 28th it was discussed, then rejected. On May 30th we announced our departure, then reversed it. The main reason was that non-Beijing students were not prepared to leave. It meant that anyone who was prepared to stand as a spokesperson had to confirm the occupation of the Square. The situation is now out of control, and we are waiting, active, for the government's response.

Second Interview

Question: The situation in Beijing is very dangerous now, so I hope that this is not the last time that I can talk to you. Why did you get so involved in the Movement, becoming a student leader?

Answer: I have cared about the democratic development of China for some years. I even wrote articles, but these were not published. Now I think that we have a great Student Movement; and I feel that I have the energy and ability to devote myself to playing a leadership role.

Q: What's your opinion on the death of Hu Yaobang?

A: The death of a citizen, even of a communist, never causes much excitement; which is perhaps a problem in itself. The fact that the death of this democratic leader has led to such immense chaos shows just how unsatisfactory the situation is in China.

Q: What were your hopes upon joining the Movement?

A: Two things. First, I wanted it to be like the May Fourth Movement, and improve democratic consciousness. The Chinese have a thirst for democracy, but they lack an understanding of it. Through the Movement educational work could be promoted. Second, I hoped that we could set a good example of the skills required for democracy. At first, I had hoped that the Autonomous Students' Union of Beijing Universities (ASUBU) could gain legal status and form an opposition to the government.

Q: What were the government's errors in dealing with the Movement, and what issues developed in consequence?

A: Before the big demonstration on April 22nd students aged 18 or 19, with no proper organization, made various appeals. At that stage, if the Government had really wanted to, it could easily have handled the issue.

Q: Given the government's determination, what became the goals of the Movement?

A: One cannot be sure, but I don't think that the situation will turn into chaos.

Q: What were the other errors of the government?

A: On April 22nd the police and soldiers attacked the students. That united the students, and led to the Temporary Students' Union of April 27th. The Student Movement became markedly different as large scale organizations were set up.

Q: What do such errors tell us about the government and the future?

A: I think that the basic cause of these errors was the undemocratic attitude of the government. It is not familiar with democratic activities, like demonstrations. Its own decision-making is not democratic. In fact, all matters are decided by one person. Even Li Peng said that the Government was controlled by Deng Xiaoping. The lack of democracy and hostility to the democratic way of life is the main reason for the current situation. At the same time, another problem is the poor quality of the leaders in the top ranks of the Government.

Q: What are your motives in leading the Movement? What conceptual ideas do you use to understand democracy and the present Chinese society?

A: My motives are simple. I'm extremely dissatisfied with the society. I study Education, so I analyzed the problems there, and discovered that the situation was very serious. I recognise that solutions cannot be provided by a bad political system. Therefore, our Student Union has to promote political reforms. First, we demand protection of our rights and freedoms as defined in the Constitution. We also seek a guarantee on the continuation of economic reforms and freedom of the press. There are many problems in China's system, including corruption, bureaucracy, and dictatorship. The major problem, however, is the fact that people cannot exercise their political rights, cannot control their political and economic lives. In fact, this is a Democracy and Human Rights Movement.

Q: Has there been a personal development for you in your experience of continual dialogue and participation in a large social movement?

A: Of course. My analytical skills and powers of observation have increased considerably. This is better than reading books. I also learned that there are practical problems inside the society and the government. These may not be noted by ordinary people. For one thing, democratic consciousness cannot exist without the right environment and the people. As I have said, the greatest barriers to progress are our one billion people and five thousand years of Chinese history.

Q: From your experience in the Movement, what is China's major problem on the road to democracy?

A: There are two aspects:

1) The democratic consciousness of the people. We are promoting democracy, but the people say simply, "Li Peng step down!" The latter is not a democratic mentality.

2) Systemic hindrances mean we cannot fully promote the democratic consciousness. If the government insists upon rejecting the creation of an opposition party, there will be no counteracting political force, and no hope for reforms and democracy in China.

Q: If your theories are applied, what will be the government's response? What is the probability of your success?

A: I think we will surely win, but it's difficult in the short run. In the long run, democracy must be developed, and our actions promote this. At present, our strength is not great and we have to work harder.

Q: What are the systemic problems?

A: Looking at things in Beijing over the past couple of days, nobody could be very optimistic. We must face reality. There may occur a serious drawback to the development of democracy.

Q: My view is that the next two to five years are crucial, irrespective of government violence or whether or not Li Peng is in power. Given that, if you are free, what will you do?

A: Try to establish a political opposition. I agree, however, that Li Peng may step down, and that there could be another purge within the party.

Q: Besides the government, have you discovered any problems among the students and the public?

A: We lack the experience of democracy, or we are too deeply influenced by the bureaucratic system. In fact many student leaders are quite bureaucratic, which is a great obstacle.

Q: What is your view of the political movements of the last forty years? For example, how do you think of the May Fourth Democracy Wall Movement of 1986-1987? Have you any general comments?

A: There's no basic difference between the past and present Student Movements. In the past, however, it lacked organization, the numbers were smaller, and they could not generate the agreement and support of people. This time our greatest success has been to achieve a consensus and reaction among the citizens of Beijing, building up a great countervailing power. We're still not satisfied, and it's hard to make progress. We may lose on this occasion; but very soon another Student Movement will appear on an even larger scale, and it will be more successful.

Our generation has witnessed the open-door foreign policy of China. The contributions of Hu Yaobang and others made us become more open-minded. After this event, the university students in the nineties will have a stronger sense of democracy.

Q: We know from the newspapers that many intellectuals declared support for you, and also promoted your political ideas. Can you point out the difference between you and them?

A: In China, a few young people have done a lot for democracy. I think the young ones are more educated than the elders, and are also pure in mind. Because of the environmental influence of the feudal system for thousands of years, the intellectuals are usually compromising and weak. They may have some suggestions. But what China needs now is specific ways to strengthen the sense of individualism in the citizen. This is not just a concept, but something which must be practiced. To do this, we think the young ones are stronger and purer.

Q: My view is same as yours. For the last ten years I have noticed that intellectuals, especially those who pursued democracy and freedom, concentrated mainly in the conceptual areas. Unlike you, they did not get away from existing society.

A: Yes, you're right. Their ideas usually agreed with the so-called reformists. My view is that we don't need reforms. We have had reforms in the past, even as far back as the Qing Dynasty, but they have never succeeded. Reforms are useless. China needs revolution. Of course I don't mean a military revolution. What I mean is: intellectuals think the power should remain at the top, with Government; but it should lie among the people.

Q: What is your definition of the "people"?

A: The people cannot be treated as a single whole. It is individuals, or organizations. The people is composed of every citizen. The old concept views people as identical, but this is an insult. We must recognise complexity, which is completely different from treating one billion individuals as a single group.

LXVII: An Interview With Chai Ling [4]

Question: What is the significance of Tiananmen Square to the Student Movement in Beijing?

Answer: We can say that the Square was a symbol to the Student Movement, especially before May 13th. Since May 13th, the first day of the hunger strike, the Square has been the focus and symbol of all the Chinese people, and of everyone in the world who seeks democracy.

Q: How do the masses see Tiananmen? Does it look to government, to Maoism, or to a new China?

A: We have often heard that the masses look to the students with admiration. They identify the students with their own sons and daughters, fighting for their own interests. The transformation of the Student Movement to a Democracy Movement indicates that the Chinese people are exerting their authority, that a new China is born, one which belongs to the people.

Q: What has the atmosphere been like over the past few days?

A: There have been some management problems and some confusion; but the organization is very united, and we are confident.

Q: What are your plans now?

A: I have seen some of the bad traits present in the Movement, and have been distressed by them. I have thought of quitting. I dearly wished for competent people to come forward to lead the Movement; and it should have been able to produce other people like myself.[5] Then, I realised that this might not happen; and in the absence of persons worthy of my trust, that I should stay on. To do otherwise would be a sin against the Movement, and so I decided to remain as Commander-in-Chief, which I still am.

Q: Do you think that Deng Xiaoping, Li Peng or Zhao Ziyang are making use of the Movement?

A: Naturally. Every Movement in the past has produced governmental changes. However, the present Movement has been unique in putting itself above factional struggles. We will not get involved in them, even though they attempt to use us. Such attempts are, I think, in vain; for the aim of the Student Movement is to struggle for progress towards a modern Chinese democracy. The Movement does not choose between Li or Zhao; for we oppose every leader who stands in opposition to the people. If, however, a leader takes a popular position, reflecting the demands and interests of the people, then he will be supported by them.

Q: You place the greatest emphasis on democracy. There are probably many Chinese who don't understand what it is. In the United States, democracy means the choice of each new President by popular vote.

A: I think that democracy is a natural right. In the past, human nature in China was very restricted, and there were no rights. For example, consider the conditions in the universities. When it comes to getting a job, you must go where the party decides. Furthermore, there is no supervision over the party, the security forces, or the army. This gives rise to profiteering, corruption, decadence and all of the ills that have accompanied the last ten years of economic reform. Those who acquired wealth recently all have links to those in power. The Chinese have had an emperor to rule them for more than two thousand years. There has never been freedom of speech, freedom of the press, or personal security, and there is little hope for the future. Prior to this Movement there was a moral crisis, and nobody was interested in anything but money. Through this Movement the Chinese have regained a sense of purpose and ability to solve their own problems. We do not depend upon foreign models, but upon ourselves.

Q: Can democracy and communist-socialism co-exist?

A: I have not done any great theoretical research. My view is that democracy is a basic human need, and not contrary to the basic tenets of communism. The sort of democracy which we demand is very natural, a natural right. It is not hooked up to any specific ideology. We are fighting for control of our own lives.

Q: Do you visualise how democracy will spread in China?

A: I think that it will be a long process, possibly sixty or seventy years. My hope is that one day we might live securely in a China where people can enjoy the fruits of their labours whilst possessing the power to participate in the management of the country. We shall have power to determine the policies implemented by our leaders, feeling ourselves to be our own masters in a country that we own. It will be a powerful nation which each generation will struggle to maintain.

Q: Will your Movement have any international significance?

A: Knowledge has no barriers. Although we struggle for our own country, we can have an influence on others as members of the world community.

There has been some confusion, but the more resolute of us are now united to combat that. We have demonstrated to the world that we are orderly, reasonable and strong. I say to you from the bottom of my heart that, if this Movement fails, it will be a tragedy for the whole nation. It will mean that the people's democratic consciousness was insufficiently developed, and that it was doomed from the start. The few thousand students on the Square cannot alone prevent its failure. However, if the Movement succeeds, the victory for democracy will be a liberation of the human nature of the whole Chinese people.

Q: Are your ideas similar to those of the May Fourth Movement? Are you the descendants of the revolutionaries of that period?

A: We have inherited some things from the May Fourth Movement. There are also differences. History will judge.

Q: In the May Fourth Movement both democracy and science were important.[6] What is the importance of science to you?

A: For us, only after democracy has blossomed will science be guaranteed. I read science at university. I would argue that up to this point in time such studies have been useless, and the prospects for China hopeless. Every strata of society saw no hope for the country. Science and technological knowledge have to be converted into productive force, which cannot be done if there is no guarantee of democracy.

Q: Do you want to see a country of equality or inequality of wealth?

A: We don't have statistics; but I would say that the disparity of wealth in China today, between the privileged and the ordinary person, is as extreme as that found in capitalist countries. I would hope that, after human nature is liberated in our society, a kind of spontaneous and harmonious regulation will occur. There will be differences. For example, those who are wise and hardworking will be better off than the lazy and incompetent. This is a natural inequality and not deliberately designed. However, today China's inequalities are deliberately produced by those in power, man-made and unnatural.

The Movement has been spontaneous and non-conspiratorial. There is no ruling theoretical framework. We just follow our feelings! It is a pure and unsullied demand for democracy. In it we see that the best and most advanced elements are students, who form a vanguard for the nation.

June 3, 1989

LXVIII: *An Interview with Fang Lizhi* [7]

Question: Professor Fang, recently Hong Kong newspapers disclosed some high level internal documents of the mainland government. Yang Shangkun gave a speech on May 24th at an extended emergency meeting of the Military Commission [of the CCP], saying that the older leaders had concluded that the Student Movement had its roots within the party. This seemed to imply that there was a link between intra-party struggles and the Movement. Do you agree?

Answer: The Student Movement, especially at the start, was entirely spontaneous. That it has since been infiltrated is a possibility. Nonetheless, the students made a spontaneous call for democracy. If we look at Yang's statement in a few years we will see that he greatly distorted the character of the Movement.

Q: In your view, how does the Student Movement differ from the Cultural Revolution?

A: The Cultural Revolution was a movement initiated by the leadership from the top downward. From the first big character poster the Cultural Revolution was a manipulation of the masses by the leaders, later developing into an inner-party struggle. This time the movement moves upwards from the base, urging the leaders to change and make reforms.

Q: But Yang Shangkun said that there were two commanders of the Student Movement in the Politburo, and that Zhao Ziyang had attempted to split the party.

A: (Jocularly) That at least shows how limited their vocabulary is. I cannot say at this time whether or not Zhao Ziyang is "splitting the party." However, compared with the Soviet leaders, the mentality of China's leaders is primitive. In the USSR differences at the top levels of the party are made public, indicating a degree of openness and confidence. If one is frightened of disclosing one's own problems, it shows a lack of confidence and weakness.

Q: Government officials gave examples to illustrate how the Student Movement was re-enacting the Cultural Revolution; for example, it pointed to the millions of people demonstrating on the streets.

A: The Cultural Revolution was a movement in which the leaders hoodwinked the masses. The Student Movement this time is a spontaneous one that grounds itself in the independent judgement of a large number of people. Other comparisons are meaningless. It is like the party saying that it is against all wars, and then advocating "just" wars, when it is obvious that all wars are equally cruel.

Q: The Secretary of the Beijing Municipal Council, Li Ximin, criticised you at a meeting of the party cadres, Politburo and Military Commission on May 19th for saying that the people would take to the streets before long. Did you ever make such a remark?

A: I might have. I was asked if a discussion at a meeting had been heated, and replied that it had, and that people would shortly be taking to the streets. I was simply commenting on the character of a meeting.

Q: On what occasion did you make the remark?

A: Privately, to a few people, or perhaps over the phone during a meeting. It was not a public statement, so it must have been reported by a spy.

Q: They also thought that Zhao Ziyang's supporters were enlarging the Movement.

A: I don't know, but I feel that many of them shared the same views, particularly during the early stages of the Movement.

Q: Li Ximin also emphasised the foreign influence on the Movement.

A: More nonsense!

Q: Yuan Mu also suggested that only Fang Lizhi himself knew what role he was playing.

A: (Laughing) This is the language of struggle of the Cultural Revolution. Could I but be the instigator of such a large-scale movement I would feel very, very honored. How honorable it would be to be capable of instigating millions of people to raise their voices in a cry for democracy.

Q: Having spoken with you the Taiwanese authoress, Long Yintai, said that you had been "on the alert to avoid suspicion." Was that because you feared that others would accuse you of being the "Black Hand" behind the Student Movement?

A: My being alert is not because I have something to fear, but because I want the students to take the more active role. They want to act, and do not need my interference in their autonomy. This shows that, in China, it is not simply "a very, very small minority," such as Fang Lizhi, who ask for democracy.

Q: They repeat the word "zui" [denoting a superlative when used before an adjective] when referring to "a small minority."

A: This is the parroting of the language style of the Cultural Revolution. The repetition of "zui" five times was the innovation of a student at the Second Girls' College in a speech of congratulation to Chairman Mao. So it is not an invention of the present leaders.

Q: It is also said that Fang Lizhi is on the alert, but his wife, Li Xian, often mixes with students, and is not above suspicion.

A: She is a lecturer at Beijing University, so it is natural for her to be with her students. For her not to be with them would be abnormal. Moreover, she is a representative of the University in the National People's Congress. So it is both her duty and her obligation to be in touch with the students.

Q: Is it also her duty to be involved in the off-campus campaign?

A: She should respond to student requests, which is her duty. However, last month she was discovered to have heart disease. So of late she has done nothing at all. Following Hu Yaobang's death some students contacted her, but she didn't go to Tiananmen Square. She went to the university, naturally; but reports that she joined in the demonstrations are mistaken.

Q: Is there any direct or indirect influence from the intellectuals on the escalation of the student movement?

A: Yes, of course. But it is chiefly ideological influence. Since the beginning of the year, intellectuals have put forth demands for an amnesty for political and ideological prisoners, and have held several academic discussions. All these had some influence on student opinion; but I don't think that intellectuals have influenced the actual organization and arrangement of the campaign. At most there is the possibility that students consulted them; but I don't think that the connection is strong.

Q: Why has the slogan, "Amnesty for Political Prisoners," not been heard in the Student Movement, which seems indifferent to the signature campaign [for the release of those incarcerated in 1979]?

A: Twenty-year old students actually don't even know who Wei Jingsheng is. Compared with older people, students are less concerned about political prisoners. What concerns them is government corruption and freedom of the press. If you trace the origin of their thoughts, they are similar to ours; it is just their slogans that are different.

Q: After the May 4th demonstration the students returned to their classrooms. What was it that gave rise to the hunger strike campaign on May 13th?

A: On May 4th Yuan Mu said that a dialogue was needed; but there was no dialogue. Maybe he thought that it could be delayed indefinitely. Everyone in Beijing knew that there was still a problem, and nobody was surprised when the students rose up again. It was the hunger strike that was a surprise.

Q: A hunger strike is a powerful and new weapon.

A: At the beginning, especially on the second day when someone declared that he was going to set fire to himself, the atmosphere was very tense. We discouraged them, saying that it would be better not to stage a hunger strike.

Q: Was the hunger strike and its timing entirely the students' idea?

A: Most likely. It is also evident that it was staged for the visit of Gorbachev.

Q: Taking place when the whole world was watching the Sino-Soviet summit, the hunger strike embarrassed the high ranking government officials. We can easily imagine how angry they were. Were the students interfering deliberately?

A: I think that they expected larger numbers of reporters, local and foreign, during that time, thus creating a bigger impact. That was all. They just wanted a dialogue with officials who have decision-making power. It is no use having discussions with people like He Dongchang.[8]

Q: Li Ximin stated that overseas Chinese had made a statement at Columbia University, proposing that you be the leader of an opposition to the CCP. Is that so?

A: I know absolutely nothing about it.

Q: We know from Li Peng's speech that the government condemns the student movement for advocating a multi-party system in China. Do you think that this is the ultimate goal of the movement?

A: The student movement aims at establishing a democratic society. Concerning the degree of democratization, I don't think that the students have very clear ideas. The present consensus is to fight for freedom of the press, freedom of speech, and to solve the problem of corruption. As to whether the next step is to amend the Constitution and to have Soviet style elections, no satisfactory discussions or conclusions have been realised. I rarely went to listen to the student discussions at Beijing University. There were certainly discussions of a multi-party system on big character posters, but the main question was the demand that their autonomous organization be regarded as legal. That is very important, for it relates to the future development of independent organizations.

Q: Are the authorities soon going to break up the student organization in Tiananmen Square?

A: It's difficult to say.

Q: Should the students retreat from the Square?

A: It is difficult for me to say. Certainly they should understand, as I have often told them, that the struggle for democracy takes more than one or two months. I warned them not to let their health deteriorate, as democracy requires a long struggle, and cannot be attained by a single act. It might even take a generation, with extensive preparation.

Q: If the students retreat without a dialogue, without a renunciation of the April 26th editorial, and without Li Peng stepping down, will the movement have been a failure?

A: Not a failure. Rather an ebbing of the tide. Even if you call it a failure, one should not underestimate the impact of the Movement. It is not simply a conflict over the April 26th editorial. Since the liberation forty years ago, this has been the first time that a Movement has made the masses realise that government is properly regarded as a servant of the people, open to criticism. This is a remarkable step forward, an unprecedented achievement, crucial to the democratization of China. In its final form democracy can involve a multi-party system. What is more important now is to cultivate a psychological attitude and popular lifestyle that gives everyone the right to criticise the government. The Student Movement has had a tremendous influence in this direction.

Q: Some think that the Student Movement should be replaced by a Workers' Movement. Are you optimistic about this?

A: This time workers have already joined the Movement. Not many, and they are not as well organised as the students; but the

Movement has influenced the workers, particularly the young ones, which cannot be underestimated.

Q: Is a Solidarity Movement likely in China?

A: It is not absolutely impossible.

Q: Are you optimistic?

A: Not very. But the workers do have some of their own organizations. As to their maturity, we just don't know yet.

Q: The government officials seem sensitive to the possibility.

A: As they are to the student organizations.

Q: Is it possible that the Movement could achieve a greater press freedom?

A: Laws concerning the press are to be discussed on June 20th. This could well be the one small positive result that the Movement can achieve.

Q: Could similar movements, challenging specific policies, gain like concessions?

A: Possibly. In the past, whatever you opposed got worse, as increasing numbers of people were accused of having "polluted minds" and of being "bourgeois liberalizers." To consolidate its position the leadership had no choice but to be high-handed. Under pressure from the masses, however, the leadership itself may get polluted and liberalised.

Q: I remember that you once told reporters that Deng Xiaoping and Li Peng must step down. Is this still your position?

A: I have long said that Deng should resign. As for Li Peng, he has failed. As Director of the commission for education he achieved nothing over a long period of time, as they have admitted themselves. As Premier, he has done nothing of note.

Q: Suppose Li Peng steps down, is there a better person to replace him?

A: I can't give you a name right now, but there are certainly better people available.

Q: What are your views on Zhao Ziyang?

A: In the sphere of economics, Zhao has indeed carried out reforms. As for reforming the political system, he did less than Hu Yaobang.

However, he does seem to be prepared to deal with the Student Movement and go ahead with political reforms.

Q: People overseas have heard rumours about Zhao's demise, with accusations that he has ignored his son's corrupt activities. Any comment?

A: This might be true.

Q. Recently, people here have been concerned that the Government will take revenge upon the participants in the Movement. How likely do you think this is?

A: The scope and duration will depend on the circumstances. If they can get even with the people, they will do it. It depends.

Q: Can you take a guess?

A. It is their intention to get even with the people. For them, that is a definite must. Can they actually do it? How will they do it? That all depends upon the circumstances.

Q: Can you say for sure that there will be an element of revenge?

A. Yes, of course.

Q. At this time only two people have been named by them: Fang Lizhi and Ren Wanding. Will you be the first target?

A. Very likely.

Q: How are you preparing for this?

A: (Laughing) I'm not.

Q: Are you worried?

A: I'm not un-worried; but if the democratization of China requires sacrifices, so be it. The Chinese people are firm, and we are not afraid of official authoritarianism.

Q: Recently circulated blacklists show the number of people to be arrested as varying from twenty to more than a thousand. We also hear that the number of Solidarity members arrested in Poland now adds up to about a thousand. Is this credible?

A: The different figures are different policy options of the government. As to the one which they will adopt, I can only say again, it depends on the circumstances.

Q: By circumstances you mean the struggle of the masses, and the power struggle at the top.

A: First, the power of the masses, and how many are prepared to follow. Then, naturally, the power struggle.

Q: It is now widely thought that the authorities have shifted their focus from the Student Movement to the intra-party struggle. Has the conflict between Li Peng and Zhao Ziyang reached an end? What do you expect?

A: It is difficult to speculate, for in China the upper echelons operate behind closed doors. Compared with people like yourself, we know so little.

Q: Professor Fang, many thanks. I hope that this will not be our last interview.

A: (Laughing) It doesn't matter even if it is.

NOTES

1. These interviews were conducted by an unnamed fellow student on June 2, 1989. The introduction is an assessment by that student of Wuer's relationship to his fellow activist in Tienanmen Square, Wang Dan, and a comment on Wuer's background and personality. Wuer escaped to the USA via France after the June repression. Wang was arrested in July 1989.

2. These comments are apparently made to counteract suggestions that Wuer was receiving funds from (and being influenced by) western reporters, who could be thought to be anti-socialist sensation seekers.

3. Wuer's distrust of the intelligentsia mirrors the traditional distrust of that group by the CCP. As was indicated earlier, the intellectuals were called the "stinking ninth" after the other specified "class enemies," who were: i) landlords, ii) rich peasants, iii) counter-revolutionaries, iv) "bad elements, " v) rightists, vi) renegades, vii) enemy agents, and viii) capitalist-roaders.

4. Transcript of an interview with freelance American journalist, Phil Cunningham, June 3, 1989. Chai Ling was one of the four high profile student leaders — with Cheng Congde (her husband), Wuer Kaixi, and Wang Dan.

5. To be identified as a leader or organiser of the Movement obviously carried significant risk (such as ejection from the university and imprisonment or exile) even before the massacre. It should be remembered that people like Chai Ling were self-selected, putting themselves forward, and taking on the tasks. That they were followed was often the measure of their popular support, although elections were also held at mass meetings. We see her taking the mantle of leadership, as she describes it here, at the time of the May 13th hunger strike, in which she participated. She is also saying that she would like other people to do the same, and that not all those who took on organizational tasks were honest and/or competent.

6. The question of science has many implications in the PRC. As a vehicle for industrial modernization it is important. However, those who possess scientific credentials have

often been accused of being elitist. In the years of Mao's dominance, one of the slogans was "Better Red than Expert." We had in the sixties the interesting picture of China's nuclear scientists saying that they only succeeded in producing their bombs because of the inspiration of Mao's thoughts. We should also remember that Marxism-Leninism-Maoism claims to be scientific communism, a claim which many social and physical scientists dismiss as inappropriate; but in doing so challenge the legitimacy of a one-party rule. Finally, we should note that communist regimes have been faced with bureaucratic inhibitions to the introduction of new methods and technologies, especially when they required autonomous decision-making being given to their operators.

7. The physicist and human rights activist, Fang Lizhi, was interviewed by telephone on May 31, 1989, by a representative of the Hong Kong journal, *Liberation Monthly.* Fang took refuge in the embassy of the USA at the time of the massacre. His incarceration was otherwise inevitable, as he indicates here.

8. A low-ranking official who had met with student representatives, and to no avail.

WITNESSES TO THE MASSACRE

LXIX: Chai Ling's Sense of Foreboding [1]

These might be my last words, for the situation becomes ever more serious. I am now twenty-three years of age and, coincidentally, my birthday was the day Hu Yaobang died this year. I am from Shandong province, and I came to Beijing in 1983 to study psychology. In 1987 I was admitted to Beijing Normal University to undertake further studies in child psychology.

On May 12th I made a speech in which I said, "Our generation has the courage to die. We don't want that, preferring to win and to live under the clear skies of a reformed republic." One teacher told me that my speech had brought him to tears.

At 7:30 p.m. on May 13th, we met the others at Beijing Normal University, and went to the Square to begin the hunger strike. That evening there were less than a thousand of us; but the numbers were later to increase to more than three thousand.

It is asked: Is your action inspired by Gandhi? Indeed, I had thought of this; for when demonstrations and petitions do not work, one must offer one's own life to attract the attention of others, and to move the situation forward. I was very anxious, with a sense of great responsibility for the participants. However, even after Wuer Kaixi and others of our representatives had met with Yan Mingfu, we rejected requests to abandon the hunger strike.

Li Lu said to me that if the government ignored the strike, then we should adopt even more aggressive tactics, and set ourselves on fire. Speaking from the podium in the Square, I said that I was ready to take the role of Commander-in-Chief of the Hunger Strike Group, and sacrifice myself in order that other students might live on. Later I saw unconscious students taken away in ambulances, and I felt absolutely depressed.

There was an attempt to enter the Great Hall of the People. Knowing that the security forces would take some time to arrive, I begged those hunger strikers who had the strength to stop those involved. The leadership of ASUBU then arrived to stop it. There was chaos; for some of the student leaders were not motivated by good intentions.

I felt that the Hunger Strike Group should take the lead, having been present throughout. Since adopting a leadership role I had noticed that various organizational tasks were not being carried out. There had been 182 people in various positions; meetings were convened without serious thought or purpose; the health of the students deteriorated; requests for food got less response; and sanitary conditions became terrible. Worst of all, the students were becoming short-tempered as tension mounted in response to events.

Students from all parts of the country continued to arrive in the Square, and were frequently disappointed. Many of them did not know what we were struggling for, and had come along just for the ride. I heard that some students kept money donations for themselves; and some agreed to be interviewed by reporters only if they were paid. Worst of all, some students made a deal with the government, agreeing to retreat from the Square in return for merit marks on their records. As to the numbers of informers, we have no solid evidence.

Yet the darkest day has still to come. Many students don't understand that staying in the Square is the only way left for us; if we retreat, the government will be delighted. As Commander-in-Chief I refuse to compromise. Meanwhile we see the Autonomous Union of Non-Beijing Universities and the faction which preaches surrender competing for power with ASUBU. There are many who make use of the Movement to promote their own egos — people like Liu Xiaobo.[2]

I think that the Government will retaliate upon every one of us in a crazy manner; for the Chinese have a strong orientation towards revenge. Therefore, I have no unrealistic hopes. After our first dialogue [with party leaders] was broken off, I read out our declaration on the hunger strike, hoping that it might be broadcast over all the country, so that people would know why we had undertaken it. We thought that we could influence them.

Many people who have joined the Movement possess no views, have confused thoughts. The Movement's purpose is to show our understanding and concern for democracy. The intellectuals and the theorists are lagging behind, not having put forward a single well-rounded argument. The Movement's greatness will be that it is the catalyst of the spontaneous rising of the masses.

I think that it is inevitable that the existing situation must change. As an individual I want to live and to see the great revolution that I believe must occur, and which I want to be part of. If I live, I want to see the people of China really rise up.

Talk of reform has brought the intellectuals to a dead end. Unless the people choose to save themselves, there will be repression. On May 25th, I was chatting to a plain-clothes policeman, and he told me that anyone arrested would be sentenced to between three and seventeen years in jail. When released from such a sentence, I would be forty. I cannot accept that. I think that the establishment of a system of democracy, and the use of scientific knowledge for the public welfare, will benefit every Chinese. Of course, we could escape abroad; but if our country can solve its problems, we would not have to spend our youth and our talents on foreign countries. My mother country is poor, and needs many people who will struggle and sacrifice for her. The trouble is that, with the current political system, people from all classes have no alternative to emigration.

Someone must unselfishly continue with the task; for the fate of the entire country is at issue.

May 1989

LXX: *The Massacre in Tiananmen Square* [3]

I am a twenty-year old student of Qinghua University. Last night I sat on the steps of the Monument to the People's Heroes and witnessed the whole incident in which the army shot the students and the citizens.

Some of my schoolmates were shot dead. My clothes are still stained with their blood. As an eyewitness and survivor, I disclose what I saw during the massacre to all kind and peace-loving people.

In truth, we knew that the army would actively suppress us yesterday afternoon. A person called on us at 4:00 p.m. and told us that the army would use violence to clear everybody from the Square. After we were told this we discussed the matter urgently. We decided to adopt some measures to alleviate the conflict and to avoid great bloodshed.

At that time we had 23 guns and some bombs, which were obtained from the army during the conflict which occurred in the previous two days. The Autonomous Students Union of Beijing Universities (ASUBU) decided to give these back to the army to demonstrate our principle of "Promoting Democracy by Non-Violence." Last night we contacted the army under the Tiananmen Wall. An officer replied that they could not accept the weapons by order of senior-ranking officials. Following that the students destroyed these weapons at 1:00 a.m. because the situation had turned critical, and these weapons might have been used as "evidence" of killing soldiers.

ASUBU announced that the situation was getting worse. Since bloodshed could not be avoided, some students and citizens had to leave the Square. But there were forty to fifty thousand students and a hundred thousand citizens who decided to remain behind. I also remained.

The atmosphere was very tense. The students had never experienced anything like this. They were certainly frightened, but they were fully prepared psychologically, their minds were firm, and many students thought that the soldiers would not open fire. Anyway, we were encouraged by a noble feeling that it was worthwhile to sacrifice ourselves for democracy and development in China.

After midnight, when two armoured vehicles sped through the two sides of the Square, the situation became much more serious. The loudspeakers of the army repeated an announcement that we should leave. Many soldiers in battledress invaded the Square from the surrounding streets. In the darkness, machine guns were set at the top of the Historical Museum.

All the students were forced to retreat to the area around the Monument of the People's Heroes. I remember that one-third were girls, and the rest were boys. Students from Beijing's higher educational institutions made up 30%, the rest being students from other provinces or cities.

At 4:00 a.m. the lights in the Square were extinguished. Again we were told to evacuate the Square. My heart pounded, as if it were saying: the time has come, the time has come. At that moment, some people who joined the hunger strike, including Hou Dejian (a popular songwriter), negotiated with the army. They agreed that the students could leave peacefully. However, when the students prepared to leave, the lights in the Square were turned on. Some red flares exploded in the sky at 4:40 a.m. I saw that many soldiers had occupied the area in front of the Square. A large group of them ran out from the eastern door of the Hall of the People. They wore uniforms, helmets and gas-masks, and carried guns. (At 6:00 p.m. on June 3rd, we had spoken with a regiment of soldiers outside the western door of the Hall. They had said that they were only a supporting regiment, and that later there would be an army from Sichuan which would deal with the students directly. Their spokesman guaranteed that they would not shoot. Therefore, the soldiers who now came out were in all probability from Sichuan).

When these soldiers appeared they assembled in a row ten or so machine guns, in front of the Monument. The gunmen all crouched down on the ground with their guns pointing towards the Monument. When this was done, many soldiers and armed police, carrying flashlights, rubber clubs, whips and various weapons, rushed towards the passive students. They attacked violently, forcing the students to separate into two groups, and move upwards on the Monument. I saw forty to fifty students with blood on their faces. Just at that moment, many armoured vehicles and soldiers moved forward. These vehicles totally surrounded us, only leaving a gap in the direction of the Museum.

The soldiers and armed police who followed us up to the third level of the Monument destroyed all our broadcasting equipment, printing machines and everything else. Then they hit the students and forced them to go down. We did not move, but held our hands tightly, singing the *Internationale* and shouting, "The People's Army would not hurt people." But the attack was so violent that we were eventually forced to move down.

When we reached the ground the machine guns opened fire. Some soldiers knelt down to shoot, and their bullets just flew over our heads. But others aimed low, and their bullets hit the chests and heads of the students. We had to go up the Monument again, then the machine guns stopped firing. But the soldiers there forced us down again. Once again we were shot by the machine guns.

Meanwhile, some workers and citizens dashed towards the soldiers brandishing bottles and clubs. Then the ASUBU ordered us to retreat outward from the Square. The time was a little before 5:00 a.m. Students then began to rush towards the spaces between the armoured vehicles. These were closed by other vehicles. Moreover, more than thirty armoured vehicles were driven at people. Some students were run over. The flagpoles were destroyed in this way. Thus the whole Square was in a state of chaos. I couldn't believe that the students were so brave. They rushed at the vehicles. Many were killed. Others stepped over the dead bodies and ran forward again. At last there was a gap, and something like three thousand students dashed out, reaching the Historical Museum. Only a little more than one thousand of these were to survive.

There were many citizens there. Together we tried to go north, but there was gunfire. So we went towards the Qianmen Gate at the south end of the Square. I was running and crying. There was a mass of students running out under gunfire. Many people fell down. When we reached Qianmen, soldiers rushed towards us from the Jewellery Market (Zhubao Shi). They carried large clubs and hit us fiercely. Many people fought with the soldiers, which allowed us to run towards the Beijing Railway Station. The soldiers chased us from behind.

It was 5:00 a.m. and the gunfire started to diminish. Later I met one schoolmate at the International Red Cross. He told me that only those who ran from the Square could have survived. The machine guns had been firing non-stop for about twenty minutes.

The most unforgettable person was one of my friends from the college. He was bleeding but kept on running with us. Later he collapsed and fell on my shoulders. He said: "Please help me!" At that time I was holding two female school friends and could not help him. He fell down on the ground. People stepped on him... He was certainly dead. Look! There is still blood on my back! There was blood covering half of his body!

I shall never forget how, when some students were shot, others recovered their dead bodies, or saved those who were injured. Some girls took off their clothes to bandage the injuries of others, until they had no more to take off.

At 6.30 a.m. two school friends and I went back to the Square. There were many people there, and we followed them to the Memorial Hall, at which point we could not go any further. There were several rows of vehicles and walls of soldiers. So I climbed up a tree at the roadside, noticing that some soldiers used large plastic bags to carry away the dead bodies of students and citizens. These were piled up and covered by a large piece of canvas.

I met a school friend who had left the Square later than me. He said that many people were dead. Soldiers even refused to let the ambulances of the International Red Cross help the injured people. We went to the First Aid Centre at the Gate of Peace (Hepingmen). We saw that many injured people were carried there by cycle rickshaws. A doctor told me that an ambulance was shot at by the soldiers and was on fire. Some injured students said that many injured students were still lying in the Square.

Around 7:20 a.m. I went back to the Square and talked with several people. They said that corpses were lying all over the Square. Soldiers covered them with cloth so that nobody could look at them. Vehicles were carrying the bodies to some unknown place. About 7:30 a.m. the soldiers suddenly shot tear gas towards the people around the Square, then they rushed towards them. I ran to the

Beijing Railway Station again. I saw several students there, all crying.

ASUBU had given us Beijing students an assignment: to lead students from other places to the Railway Station. I took them to the Waiting Room, but the staff told us that all trains were cancelled. We were leaving when some citizens approached us, saying that they would take the students to their homes for protection. Many people were in deep sorrow and cried. The citizens of Beijing are really good.

How many people were killed? I'm not certain. But I believe that some day the killers must pay!

Pessimistic? No, I'm not, because I have seen China's future in the goodness of the people! Some of my schoolmates are dead, and many are injured. But I'm alive, I know how to live, and I'll remember all of the dead students. I surely know that all righteous people in the world will understand and will support us!

June 4, 1989

LXXI: Concerning June 3-4, 1989 [4]

During the massacre of June 3-4 I was part of a student patrol, which passed by many places, including Xidan, Xinhuamen, the Beijing Hotel and the main entrances to Tiananmen Square where the slaughter was greatest. I did not stay long in any one place, which is why I saw a lot that night, too much for me to remember everything clearly. However, the picture engraved on my mind is that of an abattoir, a slaughterhouse which would shock anyone.

We had already had a warning of the bloodbath which was to occur some three days before the massacre. On June 1st, when I was at a meeting with some students, we heard reports that violence would be used. Students saw troops, in groups of ten or so, dressed in civilian clothes, come out of the Imperial Palace and the Great Hall of the People. However, their size and posture gave them away as soldiers. They surveyed Tiananmen Square, looking at the tents, making notes and taking photographs. We suspected an attack, but we didn't expect things to develop so quickly. Also, at the time, the students were totally immersed in the problems of finance and administration.

Small scale clashes between troops and civilians began on June 2nd. There were reports of looting and of troops intimidating civilians. Furthermore, an old man arrived in the square in bandages, saying that he had been attacked by either a civilian patrol squad or students. However, at the temporary hospital where we removed his bandages, we discovered no injuries. The old man said that he had been forced to perform the charade.

In addition, there were small scale anti-student demonstrations by peasants in the suburbs of Beijing. The truth was that the Beijing municipal authorities promised ten yuan to any demonstrator; and that anyone who did not demonstrate would be punished with fines. Soon after this the Beijing University students demonstrated with satirical slogans — such as, "Quash Democracy," "Combat Freedom," "Fully Support Government Corruption," and "Follow Li Peng and Earn Nine-Yuan-Nine." All of this was a prelude to the massacre, as Li Peng fabricated excuses for it by trying to create the impression that civilians were against the students.

The situation got worse on the night of June 2nd-3rd. Some troops began to break into the Square. Strange things happened. For example, trucks carrying soldiers from Xidan began to force their way forward towards the Square. They were confronted because they threatened the safety of the thousands of people in there. The soldiers then got down and ran away. Students, not aware that it was a trick, climbed on the trucks and picked up the guns which were in them, and took them to our headquarters. As soon as the Union leaders saw them, they immediately warned the students that this was a trap, and they sent the guns to the police. That night, however, the radio stated that ruffians had stolen the guns. Such is the kind of shameful, fascist tactic used to exploit the innocence of the students.

Moreover, disguised in civilian clothes, perhaps two companies of troops arrived in the Square on the evening of June 2nd. Mingling with the students, it was difficult to recognise them. However, we knew they were there, and many students became anxious. Announcements over the loudspeakers told everyone to remain calm, and the intruders later departed in groups of two or three. However, they left behind military clothing. Not suspecting a trap, some students put on the clothing, and even took photographs. Later on the radio announced that ruffians had stolen military clothing, bullets and bombs. Yet I was there, and saw what happened. It was a set-up.

The massacre began at 10.00 p.m. on June 3rd. In the Square we didn't know exactly what was happening, for the troops were still some distance away at Jianguomen and Xidan. We received news from the campuses that shooting directed at civilians had begun. A student who blocked a truck, and tried to lecture the soldiers on democracy, was shot down by dozens of soldiers. A fleet of army trucks moved from the Beijing Hotel in our direction, and a girl who tried to communicate with them, saying, "The PLA are the brothers and sons of the people," was shot dead in a fusillade. Later, Wuer Kaixi held her, weeping bitterly. But this was just one case of brutal murder.

The worst of the massacre began at 2:00 a.m. on June 4th. Tracer bullets reddened the Square, and the shooting was coming from its periphery. I waited and spoke with the close friends that I had made during the ten days that I had been in Beijing. For two hours we planned our tactics, the possibility of death, how to rush forward, distract the police, and protect the girls. Meanwhile, the machine guns had already opened fire upon our fellow students at Xidan, and the tanks were rolling towards the Square, faced only by unarmed students and citizens, their arms linked, forming a human wall against the military vanguard.

Tanks advanced, stopped, and troops climbed down from them, immediately aiming their weapons at us. Students refused to let them pass, shouting slogans like, "Down with Fascism" and "Overthrow Dictatorship." In response, the tanks machine-gunned us. The front row died instantly. The troops then opened fire, then the tanks rolled forward over the bodies of the fallen, leaving behind blood and mutilation. In the screaming and gunfire it was hard to understand it all. I was leading a rush whilst others were retreating. A student next to me fell sideways, and I grabbed at him to stop him falling. I looked, and could not recognise him as his head was smashed in. All the students I had been with were lost. I dropped to the ground and rolled back towards the crowd as a tank passed beside me.

The troops holding submachine guns fired at whoever shouted slogans. Some citizens threw bricks and stones at the armoured personnel carriers. The weapons used against us were various, including tanks, armoured personnel carriers, anti-aircraft guns, submachine guns, tear gas, iron bars, wooden clubs and bayonets.

I moved away and arrived at Jianguomen, where I saw many students being killed by gunfire. Then tanks rolled over them, and they ceased to be recognizable as human beings. It was chaotic there. There were sounds of gunfire and screaming, and it was difficult to know if those who had fallen down were dead or alive. I saw a girl student with long hair being stabbed in the chest by a soldier. After she had fallen down, the soldier stabbed her in the back until she died.

The cruellest killings were at the Xidan approach and the area opposite the Military Museum. Some students who managed to get out [from the Square] collapsed exhausted; and then tanks ran over them. Submachine guns raked through every person in their path. More than twenty girls from one of the universities were crushed to death when blocking military vehicles. Those who survived the first bullet were killed by a second or third volley.

The massacre on the edge of the Square lasted for hours. Anyone sat in the Square could hear the shooting, screaming and rumbling of tanks. The Monument to the People's Heroes was lit up with the red light of tracer bullets. By 4:00 a.m. most of those on the periphery of the Square were dead. At the same time, the atmosphere in the Square was calm. They all sat peacefully under the Monument, contemplating death, expecting it, accepting it.

I remember having said earlier at a student meeting that a massacre might be the best result that we could hope for. Now, everyone was prepared to die, so we shouted, "Fellow Students! Don't panic. We swear to die defending the Square, defending democracy and the dignity of China with our blood."

I remember shouting, "Hou Dejian, Liu Xiaobo and two others declared a hunger strike on June 2nd to support our Patriotic Movement, and they have been under the monument throughout the slaughter."

When Hou found out about the massacre, it shocked him and stirred his conscience to say, over the loudspeaker system, "Officers and soldiers imposing martial law, I am Hou Dejian, and I represent the Four-Man Hunger Strike Group. Let us speak with you to arrange the safe retreat of the students." But he was ignored. Later, weeping, Hou went with students to the martial law headquarters, pleading with them to let the remaining students, some ten thousand, leave in peace. We were shut in by soldiers, and surrounded by the dead on the periphery of the Square. He negotiated, and eventually they agreed to let us leave from the south-east of the Square, but to be quick about it.

I had witnessed many killings, including some of the hunger strikers of May. I was not angry or sad, just numb. I had no tears. I went from the periphery to the Monument, thinking on the cruelty of killings, so many of them my friends, and began to choke back tears. I could never forget the death of my friend with a shattered head, whom I lay gently onto the ground; and now I was waiting for my own death, determined to sacrifice myself with the remaining ten thousand.

When Hou returned he said, "My student friends, I have done something silly, and I hope that you will forgive me. But I also hope that you will retreat now." There was no response from us, so he continued, "We have shed enough blood, and can expect nothing from this party and government. Don't wait to be massacred, save yourself for tomorrow. Leave now."

There was dead silence. As he spoke the army was moving near, and the students were furious. A student of the Autonomous Union of Non-Beijing Students stood up cursing, "Hou, get out, you bastard! You should not have done it. Leave by yourself." and then sat down. Hou shouted to us again, but we remained motionless as the army moved towards us, raking the Monument with their bullets.

Then Wuer Kaixi spoke, saying, "My fellow students, don't just sit there. Calm down and make a decision." Hou made another appeal, saying that he knew that we were not afraid to die. Many wept. The lights in the Square went out. And then the troops were upon us.

I was in the second row. The police were confronting us. Hou made a final appeal, saying he would stay until the last student had left; and some students did stand up and move towards the south-east corner of the Square. As this happened, and as we were retreating, the police opened fire. Those with clubs beat us. Girl students were shot, their flesh torn and bleeding, their clothes ripped, trampled under soldiers' feet. The soldiers would not let us retreat peacefully, but used their guns on us instead.

There were many tents, large and small, erected by students from more than four hundred universities from throughout the country, including the [more than seventy] Beijing institutions and Hong Kong. There must have been hundreds of students sleeping in the tents, exhausted because of the many sleepless nights preceding. Having faced death every day, denied the opportunity to sleep, they fell asleep as soon as they lay down, and no sound could wake them. Many of these sleeping students were crushed to death by the movement of the tanks, there being no time to save them. Side by side the tanks rolled over their bodies, grinding them to pieces, as did the personnel carriers. If I had moved a minute later than I did, I too would have been crushed.

I was retreating at a run with some students. I saw a girl from Beijing University, her face covered with blood, clothes torn, with no shoes, lying unconscious. I rushed forward and picked her up. Guns were fired at us, those with clubs chased us.

I left the group and ran towards the History Museum. Tanks had crushed all the tents and were now circling the Square. I carried the girl up an alley. When some citizens saw us they could not control their emotions, and yelled, "Down with the fascist bastards," screaming so hard that they lost their voices. Then, as tanks approached, they took to their heels, pursued by gunfire and soldiers. I crawled along the ground with the girl in my arms. Later I settled the girl student in a citizen's home. When she regained consciousness she screamed. I helped calm her down with the residents of the household.

A report on the radio stated that a citizen was burned to death by ruffians in Jianguomen. The actual facts are these: Five heavily-armed soldiers killed many old people and children. Then, when they lost contact with the other troops, an angry crowd surrounded them. Their ammunition exhausted, the crowd rushed forward and burned one of them to death; but only after he himself had murdered many people.

As for the reported murder of a child, that was done by a soldier using a bayonet. The old chap with the child shouted, "Fascists!" The soldier then shot him dead on the spot. The child was seven years old, the man fifty-plus. They were from Henan province.

According to Red Cross estimates, more than three thousand were dead in the hospitals before I left Beijing, including not less than fifty of their own medical workers. Two research students told me that many students who had tried to give first aid were killed. Also, in addition to those crushed to death, every time a group of people had been shot, soldiers surrounded them, and no-one could see what was happening to the victims.

I was worried about getting back to school, concerned that the students would not know what was happening; so I decided to leave Beijing. However, I first wanted to send a telegram, and on the way met some angry citizens. They asked me if I was a student, and advised me to get out of Beijing as soon as possible. The fiancee of a young man who was with them had been killed. They told me that, having heard gunfire during the night, they went to the Public Security Bureau on Changan Avenue to find out what was happening. Walking in a group, speaking in a Beijing dialect, eager to ask questions and be informed, they were answered with gunshots, and the girl was killed on the spot.

When I arrived at the Telegraph Office a sign informed me that there was "No telegraph or telephone service." When I asked why this was the case the staff said, "Are you crazy? Get away from here. There is nothing that you can do." So I left, went to the railroad station, bought a ticket, and hid in the washroom.

None of the Beijing workers are going to their jobs. The army is occupying the educational centres. Soldiers are beating up students, and even those who simply distributed pamphlets are being targeted. Even when I was leaving you could still hear the sound of gunshots.

Someone has asked me to comment on the rumours that the soldiers had been injected with stimulants. Who can say? I did see a girl from the Beijing Normal University shot dead when she was trying to reason with the troops. Even old women were killed when they tried to talk to the soldiers. Even at 10.00 p.m. on June 3rd, before the start of the massacre, when I spoke to the soldiers at the entrance of the Military Museum, saying, "If you really must open fire, then fire over our heads to avoid an act of murder," a soldier pointed his gun directly at me. Not having received the order to fire, he simply said,

"Get out of here. If you don't, then I'll have to get rough."

The university student standing beside me at the time said, "Without your uniforms you are the same as us. We are both citizens, and we both suffer." The soldier, pointing the barrel of his gun at the student's chest, said, "Get out of here, or else I will shoot you." I felt that all of the soldiers were insane and inhuman. They had simply no feeling for others. They were bastards whose murderous actions would be condemned anywhere.

Women university students died miserably under the gunfire. People could not bear to watch the cruelty. Those who did not experience it cannot imagine that cruelty, with blood and remains everywhere. That blood, shed by the students, should not be wasted. Those children of the Chinese people have died for good reason, saving future generations from otherwise inevitable sorrow, making their death the greatest moment in the history of China.

I hope that all of the survivors of this bloodbath are not killed in the same way as the students, and can make the students' suffering worthwhile; i.e., utilising their strength.

Although I am still alive, I am miserable, feeling that my fellow students have died for me, that I should also be dead. This regime is prepared to kill those who know the truth, and I know what happened in the Square. I also hope that something like that will happen again, to give me the chance to die in the same cause. The citizens of Beijing know this already, but what about the other parts of China? I hope that students there will do the same thing, which is why I write now, so that they will know the truth and the infamy of the government. The students who died in Tiananmen Square should be remembered forever!

LXXII: Statement of ASUBU to Compatriots Everywhere

On June 4, 1989, one month after the seventieth anniversary of the May Fourth Movement, patriotic fighters for democracy once more soaked the flag of the People's Republic with their blood in the capital city. Blood flowed in the streets and mourning songs echoed through the city. We have reached a critical moment and must, whilst saluting the republic and the fate of those killed and wounded in the struggle, broadcast the following hard facts to the Chinese people and the world:

On April 15th [the day of the death of Hu Yaobang], the huge Patriotic-Democratic Movement was born.

On April 22nd, students in Beijing went to a rally to commemorate our late comrade, Hu Yaobang, in Tiananmen Square, in defiance of official prohibition. After the rally some students remained, kneeling before the Great Hall of the People, hoping that the authorities would accept a petition. They were simply ignored.

On April 26th an editorial in the *People's Daily* viciously described the mass movement of students as a "riot." To protest this vicious smear, the Beijing institutions of higher education organised another demonstration, for the following day. People from all parts of Beijing gave enthusiastic support. A million people took to the streets. People and students from all over the country responded enthusiastically, pushing the Democracy Movement to new levels.

Faced with popular demands and the power of the Democracy Movement, the government resorted to its usual tactics of double talk, avoiding responsibility, and trying to divide the students and the people. They refused to talk with the legitimate representatives of the students, or even discuss conditions for such a dialogue. From the first instance the students and people of Beijing handled the situation with sophistication, orderliness and restraint. In circumstances involving massive numbers of people, where the government initiated disruptive and provocative actions in the hope of creating mistrust of the movement, the protesters maintained peace and stability in the capital; and the authorities refused to listen.

On May 13th, finding the situation intolerable, one thousand students spontaneously organised a hunger strike. Within two days the number went up to more than three thousand. The whole country gave evidence of solidarity and support, demanding that the government meet the conditions put forward by the hunger strikers and engage in an open and equal dialogue with them.

On May 19th, early in the day, Zhao Ziyang, Li Peng, and other senior officials appeared in the square, speaking briefly with the students. They said that they were confident of the patriotic motives of the students, and that the party centre had never suspected us of riotous intent. They promised that there would be no retaliatory actions against the members of the student movement. *However*, on the evening of that very same day, Li Peng and Yang Shangkun sum- moned a meeting of party, military and government leaders, and came to the conclusion that the movement was indeed riotous, and that emergency steps must be taken to curb it.

The next day, May 20th, martial law was declared by the State Council [of the National People's Congress] and municipal govern- ment of Beijing. Several hundred thousand soldiers were assembled on the outskirts of Beijing, and the smell of blood was in the air.

As soon as the army moved on the city, the students and citizens flocked to the city approaches to talk to the soldiers of the People's Liberation Army. They talked to the soldiers about politics, exchanging ideas. The tension generated by the auth- orities was eased. The soldiers and the people were on friendly terms, with the citizens of this wonderful city carrying on their lives in a normal manner. According to the media, there were fewer crimes, traffic violations, and even fires, during these days. However, the planned atrocity of the government against the innocent students was under way.

On June 2nd, a speeding army truck knocked down several people in Beijing, killing three, and seriously wounding one more. The bloody suppression instigated by the reactionary government entered its preliminary stage.

On June 3rd, in the early morning, troops in civilian clothes moved towards the centre of the city on public transport. Citizens and students tried to stop them. On the approach roads to Tianan- men Square the army, using gas and rubber bullets, injured many. In one incident a seven-year-old child was stabbed to death by a sol- dier.

On June 3rd, in the evening, armoured cars, riot police, and gas were used to clear the way for soldiers who moved upon Tiananmen Square from all directions. As they progressed, the soldiers fired in- discriminately on unarmed students and citizens with machine guns and automatic rifles. Around Muxidi casualties numbered approxi- mately 400, with soldiers firing at those trying to rescue the wounded.

On June 4th, in the early morning, three armoured cars travel- ling at high speed down Xidan Road hit a bus which was in the centre of the road [as a barricade]. From the direction of the Military Museum, those in the Square could hear the roaring of trucks and continuous shooting. According to the retreating students, many of them had been killed and wounded.

In the first hour after midnight, soldiers about 500 metres down Xidan Road shot a great deal of tear gas. The crowd was forced to lie on the ground. Some cars were set afire, obviously by policemen out of uniform, with the intent of giving the authorities an excuse for carrying out a massacre. Ten minutes later, a large force of riot police, yelling, "Shoot! Shoot!", fired at the assembled civilians, who were totally surprised and absolutely vulnerable. Suddenly there were students and citizens lying everywhere on the street, dead or wounded. Those who managed to escape down narrow side-roads were shot at as soon as they were spotted by soldiers, who spared nobody, young or old.

At about 1:00 a.m. army trucks full of soldiers raced towards the end of Xidan Road. People ran up from side-roads to see what was happening, and were shot at by soldiers, who also beat those in their way with rifle butts. A student from the Second Beijing College of Foreign Languages was so badly beaten that his legs were useless bloody lumps. He also reported that five of his school-mates were shot whilst trying to rescue a female colleague. Then, some three hours later, when the soldiers had passed them, the surviving students headed for Tiananmen Square. However, the roads were blocked by soldiers who did not hesitate to open fire on the approaching crowd, even firing upon those who were running away. Where slogans were shouted, shooting followed.

From 3:00 a.m. to 6:00 a.m. on June 4th, there was a sound of shooting from Tiananmen Square and the connecting streets. Blood could be seen wherever the soldiers went by. Casualties were many, and cries and screaming filled the air. It was a horrifying scene. In the Square there were many army trucks, and tanks rolled everywhere. The preliminary estimates of dead and injured were 3000 and 7000 respectively. As the massacre continued the figure was expected to increase. Large numbers of students and citizens were drenched in blood; for they were unarmed and totally vulnerable. The only protection they had was a cloth mask, for the worst they expected was tear gas and rubber bullets. These innocent students and citizens never expected the Li Peng government to be so inhuman. From the first volley they were left wondering why they had to die. And these were the people whom the Li Peng government accused of being counter-revolutionary rioters!

Actually, what happened on June 3rd and 4th, the premeditated massacre and bloodbath, was evidence of the real counter-revolution. The people of the world will not forgive the Li Peng government the bloody debt which must now be paid.

The movement which began in Beijing on April 15th, and then spread across the whole country was honorable, patriotic, and democratic. Young students raised the banner of freedom and democracy, demanding an end to dictatorship and autocracy, which reflected the wishes of the one billion Chinese people. The movement inherited and furthered the spirit of the May Fourth Movement, and turned a new page in the struggle for freedom and democracy in Chinese history. However, a small handful who are opposed to both the party and the people, headed by Deng Xiaoping, Li Peng, and Yang Shangkun feared and hated it in the extreme. They hid the truth to protect their own interests at the expense of the people and the country. To do that they shamelessly accused this movement for democracy of being a counter-revolutionary riot. Having used threats and bribery from the beginning, they finally resorted to the bloody slaughter of unarmed students and citizens, and created a tragedy of global significance. The events reveal the horrible and corrupt nature of persons who can in no way be regarded as the government of the people. Rather it is the cruelest and most autocratic government in the world. Deng, Li, Yang and their like have shown themselves to be criminals of historic proportions, corrupted elements of our race, and the common enemies of everyone.

The fascist government has lifted its hypocritical veil and the dictators have revealed their disgusting intentions. A black cloud covers the vast landmass of China, and bloodshed fills the air of Beijing. But history has already shown that the people, democracy, and freedom will win. We, the college and university students of Beijing, will never make the slightest compromise with this evil authority, and will struggle to the end. We swear to the people of China and the world, with our youth and our blood, that we will not shame our forbears of May 4th, nor the martyrs of June 4th, nor the people of our time. At this critical moment in our nation's history, we appeal to the Chinese people to unite to overthrow the Deng-Li-Yang reactionary government, these inhuman fascists who ruthlessly slaughtered the people, these dictators who unashamedly tramped on the will of the people. We also appeal to all countries and peoples in the world who are peace-loving, and who treasure freedom and democracy, to use effective economic and diplomatic sanctions to support the Chinese students and people in their fight against the fascist atrocities of the Chinese government. Let democracy and human rights prevail. The Chinese and the people of the world must unite in the struggle for democracy and freedom. Down with autocracy! Down with fascists! Long live Democracy! Long live Freedom! Long live the People!

June 4, 1989

LXXIII: *This is How They Died in Tiananmen Square* [5]

I work for the Capital Iron and Steel Company. I arrived at Tiananmen Square at 6:00 p.m. on June 3rd to see what was going on there. Although I did not feel much sympathy for the government, I did not think that it would go to extremes. So I stayed with the students, and gave them my support.

At 1:10 a.m. on June 4th, gunshots sounded in Tiananmen. I told the students not to be frightened, that the shots would be fired in the air, and that they should neither panic nor get hold of sticks or clubs. I argued that we should talk to the soldiers and persuade them that they would meet no resistance from us; and that if we reasoned with them we could leave the square peacefully, or even be escorted out by them, with nobody hurt.

At 1:40 a.m. shots were fired. Police cars and armoured vehicles rumbled towards us from the east. At 2:00 a.m. they confronted us. I could not see if it was policemen or soldiers who fired on the crowd. At the time, everyone believed that they would use rubber bullets. I kept holding the students back and urging them not to fight, thinking that if I could restrain even one person it would be the right thing. Believing in pacifism, alone in the square, I confronted neither vehicle nor soldier; but I believed that the soldiers could be persuaded by words.

Then my faith was shattered in a burst of gunfire. The People's Liberation Army was firing at the people. The crowd was stunned to see row upon row of people falling down. They tried to get out of the way, some running wildly about, with many falling down.

As the gunfire died down trucks and armoured vehicles rolled straight towards the crowd. The Square was very crowded, and many more lost their lives.

I hid to one side, and counted the dead. In that one small spot, from 2:10 a.m. to 3:05 a.m., twenty-nine people lay in a pool of blood.

Most tragic of all were the deaths of a young woman and her younger brother. The dead boy was pulled out of a pool of blood. Seeing him, his sister lit a cigarette, and prepared to rush at the troops. The crowd restrained her, saying that the soldiers were no longer human. She promised not to do so, smoked cigarettes, until losing control of her emotions, ran at the troops.

Seeing her example, some young men rushed forwards too. At first the troops did not fire; then they shot at the crowd, and all the youths fell. The woman continued forward, ignoring her own safety. I shouted to the troops that it was a woman, and that no soldier would kill a woman. After all, she was a girl with a cigarette in her hand, not a grenade. Had the soldiers possessed any humanity, they would have arrested her when she reached them. But they shot right at her. Ten strides from the soldiers she stiffened, blood running all over her body. We rushed forward to rescue her, and where she had fallen we left a large pool of blood.

She was a tall woman, dressed in pink, in her early twenties. For her, everything was now over.

Wherever you looked there were pools of blood; and on the walls of the Imperial Palace blood stains were everywhere. Those who were wounded needed medical attention, but the soldiers did not make way. A vehicle flying a first-aid flag was prevented from entering the square by gunfire, its windows shattered. An ambulance was then denied entry. I saw with my own eyes people laying in their own blood, waiting for help, which was denied to them. Many people wanted to enter the Square to help the wounded, but they were prevented from doing so. The wounded and dying were then shot again.

What can we do in response? Nothing but a nationwide strike will be effective. Knowing what has happened, how can anyone say that the student movement is a counter-revolution? But you know what the official news report will say this morning.

June 4, 1989

LXXIV: *Chai Ling, "I Am Still Alive"* [6]

Today is June 8th, 1989. It is now 4:00 p.m. I am Chai Ling, Commander-in-Chief in Tiananmen Square. I am still alive.

I believe I am the best qualified witness to the situation in the Square during the period from June 2nd to 4th June, and I also have the responsibility to tell that truth to everyone, every single countryman, every single citizen.

At about 10 p.m. on the night of June 2nd, the first warning of what was to come was given when a police car knocked down four innocent persons, three of whom died. The second signal immediately followed when soldiers abandoned whole truckloads of armaments, military uniforms and other equipment, leaving them behind for the people and my college mates who had blocked their way. We were very suspicious of this act; so we immediately collected together everything that had been abandoned and sent them to the Public Security Bureau, retaining a receipt as proof. The third signal occurred at 2:10 p.m. on June 3rd, when large numbers of military police beat up students and citizens at Xinhuamen. At that time, the students were standing on top of cars, using microphones to cry out to the police: "The people's police love the people," "The people's police won't beat people up." Instantly, a soldier rushed towards a student, kicked him in the stomach, and scoffed: "Who loves you?" He then gave him another bash in the head and the student collapsed.

Now, let me briefly describe our position. I was Commander-in-Chief in the Square, where at that time there was a broadcasting station for the hunger strike group. I stayed there throughout, directing the activities of all the students in the Square. Of course, the commanding unit consisted of other people, such as Li Lu and Feng Zhende. We received constant and urgent messages, from every direction, that students and citizens were being beaten and harassed. That night from 8:00 p.m. until 10:00 p.m., we watched the situation get increasingly worse, as at least ten reports kept us informed of developments.

Around 7:00 or 8:00 p.m. we, the commanding unit, had held a press conference, and told both local and foreign reporters as much as we knew of the situation. There were not many foreign reporters, and we heard that this was because hotels where the reporters lived were controlled by troops, and that their rooms had been searched. So only a few foreign reporters came to the Square. The commanding unit made one statement, saying that the only slogan we held was, "Down with Li Peng's false Government."

At 9:00 p.m. sharp, all of the students in the Square stood up and with their right hands raised, declared: "I vow that, for the promotion of our nation's process of democratization, for the true prosperity of our nation, for our great nation, for defense against a handful of schemers, for the salvation of our 1.1 billion countrymen from White Terror,[7] that I will give up my young life to protect Tiananmen Square, to protect the Republic. Heads can fall, blood can run, but the people's Square can never be abandoned. We are willing to sacrifice our young lives in a fight to the death of the very last person."

At 10:00 p.m. sharp, the Democratic University was formally established in the Square, with vice-commander Jiang Deli becoming the principal, and people from all sides celebrated the occasion enthusiastically. At that time, the commanding unit was receiving many urgent warnings, as the situation became very tense. On one hand, there was the thunderous applause for the establishment of our Democratic University in the northern part of the Square near the Statue of the Goddess of Liberty; whereas along the Boulevard of Eternal Peace at the eastern edge of the Square, there was a river of blood. Murderers, those soldiers of the 27th Battalion, used tanks, heavy machine guns, bayonets (tear gas being already outdated) on people who did no more than utter a slogan, or throw a stone. They chased after the people, shooting with their machine guns. All the corpses along the Boulevard of Eternal Peace bled heavily from their chests; and all the students who ran to us were bleeding in the arms, chests and legs. They did this to their own countrymen, taking their life's blood. The students were very angry and held their dead friends in their arms.

After 10:00 p.m. we, the commanding unit, made a request based upon the principle that our Patriotic-Democratic Movement, as both a Student Movement and People's Movement, had always been to demonstrate peacefully. In opposition, therefore, to the many students and citizens who angrily declared that it was time to use weapons, we proposed the supreme principle of peace and sacrifice.

In this way, hands joined together, shoulder to shoulder, singing "The International," we slowly came out from our tents. Hands joined, we came to the western, northern and the southern sides of the Monument of the People's Heroes, and sat there quietly, with serenity in our eyes, waiting for the attack by murderers. What we were involved in was a battle between love and hate, not one between violence and military force. We all knew that if we used things like clubs, gasoline bottles and the like (which are hardly weapons) against those soldiers, who were holding machine guns or riding in tanks, and who were out of their minds, then this would have been the greatest tragedy for our Democracy Movement.

So the students sat there silently, waiting to give up their lives. There were loudspeakers next to the commanding unit's tent playing "The Descendants of the Dragon." We sang along with it, with tears in our eyes. We embraced each other, shook hands, because we knew that the last moment of our lives, the moment to give up our lives for our nation, had arrived.

There was this student called Wang Li, who was fifteen. He had written his will. I have forgotten the exact wording, but I remember him saying: "Life is strange. The difference between life and death is just a split second. If you see an insect crawling toward you, all you have to do is to think about killing it and the insect will instantly stop crawling." He was only fifteen, and yet he was thinking about death. People of the Republic, you must not forget the children who fought for you.

Between 2:00 and 3:00 a.m. on June 4th, we had to abandon our headquarters at the bottom of the Monument and move to the Monument's platform to continue our command of the Square. As Commander-in-Chief, I went with my deputy, Li Lu, to visit the students around the Monument, to give them moral support. The students just sat there quietly. They told me they would sit there in the first row, steadfast and immovable. Students in the back row said they, too, would remain steadfast. "We would not be afraid even if the front row of students was beaten and killed. We would continue to sit still and not withdraw. We would not retaliate and kill."

I chatted with the students and told them the old story that goes: "There were these 1.1 billion ants living on a mountain top. One day, the mountain was ablaze. To survive, the ants had to get down the mountain. They gathered themselves into a giant ball and rolled down the mountain. The ants on the outside were burnt to death. But the lives of many more were saved. My fellow students, we at the Square are the outermost layer, because in our hearts we understand that only by dying can we ensure the survival of the Republic." The students sang the *Internationale* again and again. They held hands tightly. Finally, the four hunger strikers — Hou Dejian, Liu Xiaobo, Zhou Duo and Gao Xin — couldn't stand it any more. They said, "Children, don't sacrifice yourselves this way." But each student was determined. The hunger strikers went to negotiate with the soldiers, with the so-called Martial Law Command Post, to tell them we were leaving. It was hoped that they would ensure the students' safety and peaceful retreat. Our headquarters consulted students on whether to leave or to stay. We decided to leave.

But the executioners didn't keep their word. As students were leaving, armed troops charged up to the third level of the Monument. They didn't wait for us to inform everyone of the decision to leave. They had already shot our loudspeakers to pieces. That was the Monument to the People's Heroes. They dared to open fire at the Monument. Most of the students withdrew. With tears in our eyes, we started to leave the Square. People told us not to cry. We said we would be back, because this is the People's Square. We only found out later, that some students still had hope in the Government and they thought that, at worst, they would be removed.

Then the tanks made "mincemeat" of them. Some say more than 200 students died. Some say more than 4000 died in the Square alone. I don't know the total. But the members of the Independent Workers' Union were on the outside. They stood their ground and they're all dead. There were twenty to thirty of them. I heard that, after the students left, tanks and armoured personnel carriers flattened tents with bodies inside.

They poured gasoline over them and burned them. Then they washed away the traces with water. Our movement's symbol, the Goddess of Democracy, was crushed to bits.

With locked arms, we went around Chairman Mao's Memorial toward the south of the Square. That was when we first saw tens of thousands of helmeted soldiers. The students ran toward them and yelled: "Dogs. Fascists." So we headed west, and saw ranks upon ranks of soldiers running toward the Square. Civilians, students, though hoarse from all the yelling, continued to shout: "Fascists, dogs, beasts." But they were ignored by the soldiers, who kept on running toward "our" Square.

We got to Xinhuamen, all of us from the headquarters in the front row. Xinhuamen was where the first bloody battle took place in the afternoon of June 3. Debris was all over the place. From Xinhuamen, we ran along the blood-slick Changan Avenue. All we saw were burnt-out vehicles, fallen concrete and debris — signs of a hard-fought battle. We later found out that, as these fascists machine-gunned people, other soldiers would pick up the dead and wounded and throw them onto buses. Some were still alive but later suffocated to death. That's how the fascists tried to hide their disgusting actions.

We wanted to go back to the Square. But the people tried to stop us. They said: "Children, don't you know they've set up machine guns over there? Please don't go back to die!" We then went north along Xidan Avenue toward the university area. Along the way, I saw a mother crying bitterly. Her son was dead. We also saw the corpses of four soldiers who had been beaten to death by citizens. We continued north, and as we neared the campuses everyone had tears in their eyes. Some people said: "Did I buy bonds to let them buy bullets to kill innocent people? To kill innocent children?"

First hand reports from students and civilians stated that these executioners acted in a calculating manner. They aimed at residential areas along Changan Avenue and fired rockets at them. Children and old people were killed. What were their crimes? They didn't even chant any slogans. A friend told me he was blocking tanks on Changan Avenue at 2:00 a.m. He saw a girl, not very tall, standing in front of a tank, waving her right hand. The vehicle rolled over her body. She was crushed into "mincemeat." My friend said the students to both his right and left were killed by gunfire. He literally came back from the dead.

On our way, we saw a mother looking for her son. She said he was alive yesterday. Is he still alive? Wives were looking for husbands, teachers looking for students. Government buildings still displayed banners calling for support of the correct policies of the party leadership. In anger, the students tore them down, and burned them.

The radio kept saying that the troops had come to Beijing to deal with riotous elements and to maintain order in the capital. I think I'm most qualified to say that we students are not riotous elements. Anyone with a conscience should put his hand on his chest and think of children, arm in arm, shoulder to shoulder, sitting quietly under the Monument, their eyes awaiting the executioner's blade. Can they be riotous elements? If they were riotous elements, would they sit there quietly? How far have the fascists gone? They can turn their backs on their conscience and tell the biggest lie under the sky. If you say soldiers who kill innocent people with their rifles are animals, what do you call those who sit in front of the camera and lie?

As we left the Square, arm in arm, as we walked along Changan Avenue, a tank charged at us and fired tear gas at the students. Then the tank rolled toward us, rolled over the students' heads, and legs. We couldn't find any of our classmates' bodies intact. Who's the riotous element? In spite of this, we in the front continued on our way. Students put on masks because the tear gas hurt their throats. What can we do to bring back those students who were sacrificed? Their souls will always remain on Changan Avenue. We who walked away from Tiananmen Square, arrived at Beijing University, still alive. Many students from other universities, students from out of town, had prepared beds to welcome us. But we were very, very sad. We were alive. Many more were left in the Square, and on Changan Avenue. They'll never come back. Some of them were very young. They will never come back.

As we entered Beijing University, our hunger strike turned sit-in, our peaceful protest, came to an end. Later we heard that Li Peng, at 10 p.m. on June 3rd, had handed down three orders: First, troops can open fire. Second, military vehicles must go forward without stopping. They must take back the Square by June 4th. Third, the leaders and organizers of the Movement must be killed.

My compatriots, this is the frenzied, puppet government that initiated a slaughter and is still commanding troops and ruling China. But my compatriots, even at the darkest moment, dawn will still break. Even with the frenzied, fascist crackdown, a true people's democratic republic will be born. The critical moment has come. My compatriots, all Chinese nationals with a conscience, all Chinese people, wake up! The ultimate victory must be the people's! Yang Shangkun, Li Peng, Wang Zhen and Bo Yibo, the final hour of your puppet regime is near!

> *Down with Fascism!*
> *Down with Military Rule!*
> *Long Live the Republic!*

June 8, 1989.

LXXV: *After The Massacre* [8]

Life seemed to be normal, undisturbed by the massacre in Tiananmen. Perhaps Guangzhou [north of Hong Kong] is too far from the site of the killings. That was the impression when I stepped down from the train on July 3rd. Friends were so excited to see me. Everybody is hungry for news from the outside world. My friend's house became a small library when others found out that I had managed to smuggle out some Hong Kong newspapers to this isolated world. Yet my friends became very cautious as more people arrived. In Guangzhou people are more open-minded and less likely to follow the government's instruction to report "counter-revolutionary activities." However, I could detect my friend's anxiety — in a community where "the Street Organization" has complete control over people's lives and keeps everybody under surveillance, only fools take things for granted.

In a mere month the atmosphere of the city has changed. It is like going back to the "old days." The propaganda machinery is in full swing again. According to the Deng-Li-Yang clique, the cause of the recent "rebellion" is a serious negligence in "ideological education" and the "toleration" given to capitalism. So "ideological education" once again becomes the core activity of one's daily routine. I tried to call a few people, but everyone was behind closed doors, busily engaging in "Studying the Speeches of Deng Xiaoping."

Prices for luxury goods such as stereos, refrigerators, and even furniture, have been slashed. Everybody is saving up for the forthcoming economic crisis. People are uncertain of the future. It is obvious that the government is short of cash. In the rural areas the government has issued IOU certificates instead of paying cash for crops. The farmers are insisting that they want cash, not bits of white paper. So it is thought that the government will start printing money next month, making inflation inevitable. Therefore, people are faced with a dilemma. If they do not spend their money now, it will become useless paper in the future. Yet the future is so uncertain that people are no longer in the "spending mood" of a few months ago. Some people are hoarding gold bars.

The streets are less crowded compared with the pre-massacre period. There are hardly any tourists from Hong Kong. The large flow of business people, migrant workers and visitors from other parts of China has ceased. People are afraid to travel. According to my friends, there have been many train accidents. Some trains were blown up, some were derailed. One train plunged into the gorges near Xion. However, the news of train accidents were suppressed along with other news so as not to further jeopardise the debilitated tourist industry.

Travellers also take the risk of being wrongly identified as one of the people on the wanted list. At every station the police search through luggage as if seeking a needle in a haystack. They also carefully match faces with those on the wanted list. We are living in a society where those who are in authority have absolute control over the fate of those unfortunates who are wrongly arrested simply because their faces resemble those of "counter-revolutionaries." They could end up in jail, or even with a bullet in the back of the skull.[9] Except for the most urgent reasons, nobody wants to travel in the environment of a spreading "White Terror." I was planning to move on to Chungdao, but my friends literally begged me not to go. "If you insist upon going, then I will risk my life by accompanying you. I will not allow you to travel alone at this time." So I cancelled my trip.

The roads are relatively quiet, the buses not crowded. I even got a seat on the bus! Life seems to carry on undisturbed. However, stories of people being secretly executed, of people failing to show up for work, of the arrest of student leaders and intellectuals, all generate uneasiness. People suffer in silent anger. Tension and anxiety are mounting.

NOTES

1. This essay was written during the May hunger strike, and its conclusion was almost illegible because of the physical exhaustion of the author.
2. Liu, born in 1954, was a lecturer at Beijing Normal University, mentor of Wuer Kaixi, arrested on June 6, 1989.
3. By "A Student Who Survived."
4. The student was a member of the Students' Autonomous Union of Non-Beijing Universities who escaped from Beijing and returned to his campus. The following is an edited recording of his statements at a meeting there broadcast by Radio-Television Hong Kong on June 22, 1989.
5. By "An Eyewitness."
6. This text was taken from a tape smuggled to Hong Kong.
7. A reference to reactionary violence by the government. The term, "White" has indicated this to all raised in Marxist-Leninist societies since the time of the Russian Civil War (1918-1921), when the Red Army of the Bolsheviks fought and won against various White Armies trying to overthrow them.
8. Reproduced from *Echoes From Tiananmen*, No. 2 (August, 1989), published by the Friends of Chinese Minshu, Hong Kong. Written by A Guangzhou resident in July 1989, after his return from Hong Kong, the author must of course, remain anonymous.
9. This is not a paranoid mentality. As Jasper Becker stated in a report from Beijing, "Security forces are routinely torturing the thousands of detainees seized in the weeks after the army crushed the student democracy movement, according to diplomatic sources... Those who die under interrogation are reported to have had an accident and quietly buried... It is not known how many have been arrested or sentenced during the past six weeks, but most estimates are upwards of 30,000." See "China reported to be torturing detainees, " *Manchester Guardian Weekly*, July 30, 1989.

BLACK ROSE BOOKS
has published the following books of related interests

Peter Kropotkin, Memoirs of a Revolutionist, introduction by George Woodcock
Peter Kropotkin, Mutual Aid, introductionby George Woodcock
Peter Kropotkin, The Great French Revolution, introduction by George Woodcock
Peter Kropotkin, The Conquest of Bread, introduction by George Woodcock
    other books by Peter Kropotkin are forthcoming in this series
Marie Fleming, The Geography of Freedom: The Odyssey of Elisée Reclus,
    introduction by George Woodcock
William R. McKercher, Freedom and Authority
Noam Chomsky, Language and Politics, edited by C.P. Otero
Noam Chomsky, Radical Priorities, edited by C.P. Otero
George Woodcock, Pierre-Joseph Proudhon, a biography
Murray Bookchin, Remaking Society
Murray Bookchin, Toward an Ecological Society
Murray Bookchin, Post-Scarcity Anarchism
Murray Bookchin, The Limits of the City
Murray Bookchin, The Modern Crisis
Edith Thomas, Louise Michel, a biography
Walter Johnson, Trade Unions and the State
John Clark, The Anarchist Moment: Reflections on Culture, Nature and Power
Sam Dolgoff, Bakunin on Anarchism
Sam Dolgoff, The Anarchist Collectives in Spain, 1936-39
Sam Dolgoff, The Cuban Revolution: A critical perspective
Thom Holterman, Law and Anarchism
Etienne de la Boétie, The Politics of Obedience
Stephen Schecter, The Politics of Urban Liberation
Abel Paz, Durruti, the people armed
Juan Gomez Casas, Anarchist Organisation, the history of the F.A.I.
Voline, The Unknown Revolution
Dimitrios Roussopoulos, The Anarchist Papers
Dimitrios Roussopoulos, The Anarchist Papers 2

send for our free complete catalogue of books
BLACK ROSE BOOKS
3981 boul. St-Laurent, #444
Montréal, Québec H2W 1Y5 Canada

Printed by
the workers of
Editions Marquis, Montmagny, Québec
for
Black Rose Books Ltd.